THE STOIC WISDOM
of
SENECA

Practical Lessons on Time, Anger, and Living Well

RICHARD LAWSON

ISBN 978-1-961963-98-6
Published by Karma Studio
info@karmabookshelf.com

Contents

Introduction

Seneca wrote for people who were busy, exposed, and under pressure.

Not for students of philosophy, but for those trying to live well while managing responsibility, ambition, loss, and emotion.

He wasn't writing from a quiet distance. Much of his work took shape during exile, political risk, illness, and the constant awareness that circumstances could turn suddenly. His letters and essays were a way of thinking in real time—clarifying priorities, correcting reactions, and steadying judgment while life continued to demand decisions.

This book approaches Seneca in that same spirit.

Rather than treating Stoicism as a system to adopt, it treats Seneca as a careful observer of how people lose time, escalate emotion, and confuse what matters with what feels urgent. His writing doesn't aim to impress or instruct. It aims to restore proportion—especially when pressure distorts it.

Each passage in this book is presented in modern English, followed by a brief explanation. The goal isn't to add interpretation, but to remove friction: to clarify what Seneca's pointing out, why it still matters, and how it connects to familiar situations involving work, family, ambition, or frustration.

You don't need a background in philosophy to read this book. You don't need to adopt a Stoic identity or vocabulary.

The reflections stand on their own. They're offered as lenses, not rules.

Throughout the book, attention is given to the areas where Seneca's most precise and practical: how time is lost, how anger forms, how ambition distorts judgment, and how consistency matters more than intensity. These themes recur not as theory, but as lived problems—ones that don't belong to any century in particular.

This book doesn't promise change. It offers clarity.

And sometimes, clarity's enough to regain steadiness.

Sources and Translation Note

The quotations in this book are drawn from Seneca's letters and essays, including *Letters to Lucilius* and selected moral writings. The original Latin texts are in the public domain and are included throughout the book.

The English renderings presented here are interpretive rather than literal. They aim to preserve meaning, proportion, and practical clarity rather than reproduce Latin structure. Wording has been adjusted where necessary to keep the sense intact and readable alongside the original text.

All selections and translations are the author's unless otherwise noted.

PART I

HOW TO READ
SENECA TODAY

Chapter 1

Who Seneca Was (and Why He Still Matters)

Lucius Annaeus Seneca was born in Corduba, in Roman Spain, around 4 BCE. He was raised and educated in Rome, where he trained in rhetoric and philosophy before entering public life. His career unfolded inside the political center of the empire, across decades marked by instability, suspicion, and shifting power.

Seneca served as senator, advisor, and eventually tutor to the young Nero. These roles placed him close to authority while leaving him exposed to abrupt reversal. Exile, recall, influence, and decline followed one another without warning. Illness accompanied him for much of his life, shaping his awareness of physical limitation and time.

These circumstances formed the background of his writing. Seneca reflected while decisions remained open and consequences uncertain. His work took shape during waiting, risk, and responsibility rather than after their resolution. Reflection, in this context, functioned as orientation. It helped him maintain proportion while circumstances continued to press.

His attention returns repeatedly to scale. Under pressure, perception narrows. Minor irritations feel decisive. Time appears scarce even as it slips away unused. Seneca's writing responds to these distortions. He examines how judgment shifts under strain and how clarity can be restored without withdrawing from action.

Responsibility remains central throughout his work. Seneca does not imagine a life freed from obligation. He considers how steadiness can be preserved while advising rulers, managing wealth, enduring illness, or waiting through uncertainty. These demands are treated as conditions of life rather than obstacles to philosophy.

Writing as Correction, Not Theory

Seneca's letters and essays function as instruments of adjustment. He watches where attention slips, where emotion accelerates, and where habit replaces deliberate choice. These moments are treated as points of failure worth examining, because they reveal how judgment operates under pressure.

His writing stays close to behavior. Seneca describes impatience while waiting, irritation during delay, confidence inflated by success, and discouragement after loss. These are not abstract states. They are ordinary reactions that arise in the course of work, relationships, and responsibility. Reflection brings them back into view before they harden into patterns.

The tone remains personal and measured. Seneca writes to friends, students, and associates who are trying to manage ambition, disappointment, and the pull of distraction. He observes these struggles with familiarity rather than distance. Experience gives his writing its authority, not position or doctrine.

Certain themes return with regularity: time misused without awareness, anger forming through interpretation, desire expanding beyond need. Their recurrence reflects how persistent these pressures are. This practice becomes a form of return—an effort to realign judgment each time it drifts.

Seneca includes himself in this process. He writes as someone aware of the gap between understanding and conduct. The value of reflection lies in noticing that gap early, while correction is still possible.

In this sense, writing serves as maintenance. It preserves clarity by keeping attention responsive and proportion intact. That practical function gives Seneca's work its steady, usable character.

A Voice Shaped by Letters

Much of Seneca's work takes the form of letters, and that form shapes how his thinking moves. A letter responds to a situation already in motion. It does not aim for completeness. It aims for clarity within a specific moment.

This format keeps Seneca's attention grounded. He writes to address impatience during waiting, unease during success, irritation in daily interaction, or discouragement during delay. Each letter begins from a concrete pressure rather than from principle. Thought follows experience, not the other way around.

The letter form also encourages precision. Seneca isolates a reaction, examines how it formed, and considers what judgment allowed it to grow. The focus remains narrow enough to stay practical. Larger conclusions emerge quietly from repeated attention to small, familiar failures of judgment.

Repetition plays an important role here. Seneca returns to the same concerns—time, anger, desire—because they reassert themselves. The writing reflects that persistence. Reflection does not close a problem. It keeps it visible and manageable.

Why Seneca Still Feels Usable

Seneca lived with tension between thought and circumstance. He wrote about restraint while handling wealth and influence. He examined simplicity while operating inside a demanding political order. These conditions sharpened his attention to cost: what success demands, what ambition displaces, and what distraction erodes over time.

This focus gives his work a practical edge. Seneca stays attentive to how pressure reshapes judgment in daily life. He observes how urgency distorts priorities, how emotion narrows perspective, and how habit gradually replaces choice. These patterns remain recognizable because they arise from ordinary conditions rather than exceptional ones.

This book approaches Seneca through that lens. His words are treated as observations meant to clarify perception, not as standards to be met. The aim is to understand what he noticed about human behavior under strain and how that understanding can steady judgment.

Seneca remains useful because the pressures he addressed persist. Time continues to slip away without notice. Emotion still escalates before reflection intervenes. Desire still expands when left unattended. His writing helps restore proportion by slowing attention and re-centering judgment.

That is where his relevance begins, and where it continues.

Chapter 2

What Stoicism Meant in Seneca's Hands

In Seneca's writing, philosophy appears as a practical resource. It's used to steady judgment in situations that demand choice, patience, or restraint. The focus remains on how decisions are made while life's already in motion.

Stoicism, as Seneca presents it, stays close to conduct. He's concerned with how people respond to delay, success, provocation, or loss. Reflection serves to clarify which reactions arise from habit and which follow from considered judgment. This distinction matters because it shapes how responsibility's carried over time.

Seneca doesn't treat philosophy as a separate domain. It enters ordinary situations without ceremony. It appears when irritation builds during waiting, when ambition presses for recognition, or when fear narrows attention. In these moments, thought functions as orientation. It helps restore proportion before reaction takes over.

What Seneca values most is judgment that remains workable under pressure. He pays attention to the early movements of emotion and the small decisions that accumulate into character. Guidance operates at this level. It refines response rather than aiming for dramatic change.

Philosophy, in this sense, supports engagement rather than withdrawal. Seneca considers how steadiness can be maintained while remaining active in work, relationships, and public life. The goal isn't distance from difficulty, but clarity within it.

Reflection as Correction, Not Perfection

For Seneca, reflection serves a corrective role. It brings attention back to how judgment has shifted in small, often unnoticed ways. The aim is adjustment rather than improvement, alignment rather than achievement.

He returns to reflection because daily life creates drift. Pressure compresses perspective. Routine dulls attention. Emotion gains momentum. Reflection slows this movement enough to make it visible. Once seen, a reaction can be weighed rather than followed automatically.

This approach keeps expectations realistic. Seneca assumes that impatience, irritation, and distraction will reappear. What matters is the capacity to notice them early and respond with proportion. Reflection supports that capacity by keeping judgment flexible instead of rigid.

Correction, in this sense, is quiet. It works without display or urgency. It works through repeated attention to ordinary moments: a delayed response, a restrained reaction, a decision made without haste. Over time, these small adjustments shape character.

Seneca values this steadiness because it holds under pressure. Reflection keeps discernment in working order, allowing choice to remain present even when circumstances press. That's its role, and its limit.

Consistency Over Intensity

Seneca places greater weight on continuity than on effort displayed in brief bursts. He watches how resolve often rises in moments of clarity, then fades when pressure returns. What lasts, for him, isn't the strength of a single intention but the reliability of judgment over time.

This emphasis shapes how he understands discipline. Consistency grows through repeated, ordinary choices made without drama. It shows itself in how time's handled, how reactions are moderated, and how priorities are preserved when attention's divided. These patterns matter because they endure beyond moments of enthusiasm.

Seneca's cautious of intensity. Strong feeling can sharpen focus temporarily, but it rarely sustains proportion. When intensity subsides, habits resume. Consistency remains available even under fatigue or strain, independent of emotional energy.

Philosophy supports this steadiness by keeping judgment aligned with reality. It provides a way to return to measure when impulse or urgency begins to dominate. Over time, this return becomes familiar. Choice remains present without requiring force.

In Seneca's hands, Stoicism serves this purpose. It offers a way to live with continuity rather than fluctuation, allowing action to remain measured even as circumstances shift.

Stoicism, in Brief

Stoicism began as a school of philosophy in ancient Greece and later developed in Rome. It was concerned less with abstract theory and more with how people conduct themselves under ordinary pressures. Stoic thinkers focused on judgment, attention, and the relationship between events and response.

At its core, Stoicism holds that external circumstances are often outside one's control, while judgment and response remain available. This distinction shapes how Stoic writers approach emotion, ambition, and difficulty. Rather than aiming to eliminate feeling, they examine how interpretation intensifies or steadies experience.

Roman Stoicism, in particular, developed in public life. Its leading figures weren't withdrawn thinkers but statesmen, teachers, and administrators. Their writing reflects practical concerns: time wasted, anger escalated, desire misdirected, and consistency lost under strain.

This book approaches Stoicism through that Roman lens, treating it as a framework for clarity rather than a system to master.

PART II

TIME:
THE ONE RESOURCE
YOU DO NOT RENEW

Chapter 3

Where Your Time Actually Goes

Seneca returns to time more often than to almost any other concern. He treats it as the pressure beneath many others. When time's used without attention, judgment weakens. When attention scatters, intention follows. What later appears as stress or dissatisfaction often begins with small losses that pass unnoticed.

Seneca approaches time through behavior rather than measurement. He watches how people give it away in familiar ways—through distraction, delay, and routines that feel harmless on their own. These losses rarely announce themselves. They accumulate quietly, until their cost becomes difficult to ignore.

Postponement receives particular attention. Plans are made, intentions stated, and life's deferred to a later moment that remains undefined. This pattern often feels reasonable while it's happening. Over time, it pushes what matters further away and turns the present into something to move through rather than inhabit.

Another pressure Seneca examines is false urgency. Activity creates the sense of necessity. Full schedules create the appearance of purpose. He separates movement from direction and asks whether effort reflects value or simply fills available time.

The reflections that follow examine these patterns from different angles. Each quote isolates a way time's lost without being felt. Taken together, they bring attention back to where time actually goes.

The aim is proportion.

"People guard their money carefully, yet treat their time as if it cost nothing."

Id agimus, mi Lucili, ut in re aliena diligentes simus, in nostra neglegentes.

What Seneca Meant

Two resources. Opposite treatment. Money gets tracked—apps, monthly reviews, passwords, worry when it's spent carelessly. Every transaction scrutinized. Every loss felt. Time? Days disappear into scrolling, pointless meetings, conversations going nowhere. Hours vanish without anyone noticing where they went. No accounting. No review. No sense that something irreplaceable just got spent on nothing.

The difference isn't reasoned—it's assumed. Money can be counted, saved, recovered. Time can't. It doesn't accumulate in an account. You can't check your balance. So it feels abundant even while disappearing. The scarcity that should make time precious instead makes it invisible.

Why This Still Matters

Your bank account forces awareness—balances, alerts, summaries. Your time doesn't. Days fill with activity, yet their shape stays unclear. You're busy twelve hours and can't name what happened.

How to Apply This Today

Open last week's calendar. Look at it like a bank statement—not to judge, but to see where the resource went. What got hours? What got minutes? What got postponed again? The pattern speaks for itself. If you wouldn't accept that spending pattern with money, don't accept it with time.

"The problem isn't that time is short, but that it slips away unnoticed."

Non exiguum temporis habemus, sed multum perdidimus.

What Seneca Meant

People complain about not having enough time. Not enough hours in the day. Not enough years in a life. The complaint frames time as scarcity—if only there were more, everything would get done. But Seneca's pointing somewhere else.

Time disappears through distraction, delay, unfocused activity. Checking your phone during conversation. Twenty minutes deciding what to watch. Saying yes to things that don't matter because you haven't figured out what does. Each instance feels minor. None announces itself as waste. But over years, these small losses accumulate into the feeling that life moved faster than you could keep up.

The problem isn't the amount of time you have. It's that so much slips away without being claimed, without being directed, without leaving any trace. Scarcity's often just accumulated waste dressed up as urgency.

Why This Still Matters

Schedules overflow. Days crowd. Yet important intentions remain untouched, meaningful work gets postponed, relationships get whatever's left over. The tension comes from effort without clarity—you're genuinely busy, working hard, staying late, answering emails at night. Still feeling like nothing that matters is getting attention.

That's because busy doesn't mean directed. Motion doesn't guarantee progress. The modern environment makes this easier than ever—there's always something demanding attention, always another message, always another task. Time gets spent reacting instead of choosing.

How to Apply This Today

Pick one thing you've been meaning to do for months. Count how many hours you spent this week on things you won't remember next month. That gap? That's where the problem lives.

"Life keeps moving while we wait to begin."

Dum differtur, vita transcurrit.

What Seneca Meant

Delay promises action later and therefore feels reasonable. You're not refusing—you're waiting for better conditions. When work calms down. When finances stabilize. When you have more energy. The delay feels like prudence.

Why This Still Matters

Many lives are organized around future phases that never arrive. After the promotion. After the kids are older. After retirement. After things calm down. These phases remain undefined, always just out of reach, functioning as permission to postpone what matters.

The present becomes a holding area. You're managing, maintaining, getting through—but not really living, not fully engaged, not doing what you'll get to later. Later becomes where your real intentions live, and it stays permanently out of reach because the conditions that would make it "the right time" never materialize.

Time doesn't pause while you wait for circumstances to improve. It doesn't accumulate like money in an account. Repeated deferral gradually replaces living with preparation. You're always getting ready, always planning to start, always one step away from beginning—and the present becomes something to move through rather than inhabit.

How to Apply This Today

Write down three things you've postponed until "things calm down." Ask honestly: in the last five years, have things ever calmed down? Has there been a month where you suddenly had extra time unused? If the answer's no, you're not waiting for the right time. You're avoiding what matters behind reasonable-sounding conditions that will never be met.

"Most people are busy without being directed."

Multos occupatos video, non multos agentes.

What Seneca Meant

Activity and intention are separate forces. Being occupied—full calendar, constant demands, staying in motion—can look exactly like progress while masking complete drift. You're doing things, important-sounding things, yet none of it's moving you toward anything that matters.

Motion fills time, but doesn't guarantee direction. Effort becomes self-justifying. You worked hard, stayed late, handled everything that came up—so the day must have been productive. Productive toward what? Progress on whose priorities?

Why This Still Matters

Modern schedules reward responsiveness over intention. Messages answered, tasks completed, calendars full. This creates the appearance of purpose—look at everything I'm handling, everything that needs me. But direction often stays unstated, assumed, inherited from whatever arrived first or shouted loudest.

Activity becomes proof of value. If you're busy, you must be important. If you're overwhelmed, you must be needed. The busyness itself substitutes for the harder question: is any of this moving you toward what you actually care about, or are you just staying in motion to avoid asking?

Without direction, busyness is just energy spent maintaining motion. You're pedaling hard, but the bike's going in circles. The effort's real. The exhaustion's real. The sense of accomplishment at the end of the day feels real. But the direction? That stays assumed, unexamined, shaped more by what's urgent than what matters.

How to Apply This Today

At the end of today, answer one question: what actually mattered in the last eight hours? Not what was urgent, not what you handled competently—what mattered? If you struggle to name three things, yesterday was busy. It wasn't directed.

"Nothing's more common than being pulled away by what feels urgent."

Ad omnia festinamus, quasi necessaria sint.

What Seneca Meant

Urgency announces itself loudly. It arrives framed as immediate, unavoidable, requiring response right now. Someone needs an answer. A problem needs solving. A decision can't wait. The pressure to act quickly narrows judgment and makes response feel automatic—like the only reasonable option is to handle it immediately.

Urgency replaces evaluation. Necessity gets assumed rather than tested. You're not choosing to respond—you're reacting to something that presented itself as requiring immediate attention. Once urgency sets the terms, judgment loses its ability to weigh whether the thing actually matters or just arrived loudly.

What makes this pattern dangerous is how reasonable it feels in the moment. Something urgent does need handling. Someone is waiting. Time is pressing. But urgency and importance are different qualities, and modern life constantly confuses them. Something can be urgent without being important. Something important rarely arrives screaming for attention.

Why This Still Matters

Your attention gets trained by what gets rewarded. Urgent things produce immediate feedback—problems solved, people satisfied, tasks checked off. Important things often produce delayed feedback, or none at all. Over time, you learn to respond to urgency and postpone importance.

How to Apply This Today

Next time something demands immediate response, stop. Just for five minutes. If it still feels urgent after that, respond. If it doesn't, you just witnessed urgency revealing itself as noise pretending to be necessity. Five minutes is enough to let adrenaline settle and judgment return.

"Being busy isn't the same as living with purpose."

Aliud est occupatum esse, aliud vivere.

What Seneca Meant

Busyness fills time. Purpose gives it shape. These are different activities, and Seneca's drawing a clean line between them.

Why This Still Matters

You can be constantly engaged—calendar full, tasks completed, people depending on you—and still miss what gives coherence to life. Purpose requires judgment about what deserves attention, not just effort. It requires knowing what you're building toward, what matters enough to protect from the constant pull of everything else.

Modern culture treats busyness as evidence of importance. If you're overwhelmed, you must be needed. If you're exhausted, you must be contributing. The full calendar becomes a status symbol, proof that your time is valuable because it's constantly claimed by others. This makes busyness easy to confuse with purpose. They look similar from outside. Both involve effort, both create fatigue, both fill days completely. But only one involves direction.

How to Apply This Today

Look at what consumed your attention this week. Don't lie to yourself, don't frame it generously—just look at where hours actually went. Now ask: did this serve what I actually care about, or did it just arrive first and demand response?

Purpose shows itself not in how much you do, but in what you choose. Not in how full your calendar is, but in whether what fills it reflects your priorities or someone else's. If there's a mismatch—if what matters keeps getting postponed while urgent nonsense gets immediate attention—you're busy. You're not living with purpose. No amount of motion will close that gap.

"We're distracted not because time is scarce, but because attention's divided."

Non quia parum temporis habemus, sed quia multum perdimus.

What Seneca Meant

The problem isn't duration. It's fragmentation. Time dissolves into small, disconnected pieces when attention scatters—five minutes here, ten minutes there, constant switching between tasks that all feel necessary. Each shift feels minor. None appears costly. But together they create a day that's technically full yet somehow empty.

Distraction doesn't announce itself as waste while it's happening. It feels like movement, like productivity, like staying on top of things. Only afterward does the cost become visible: hours passed and you can't point to anything that got finished, anything that moved forward, anything that mattered.

Why This Still Matters

Modern environments are designed to fragment attention. Notifications arrive constantly. Messages demand response. Apps compete for engagement. The technology that promises to save time instead trains attention to scatter, to check, to switch, to never fully settle anywhere.

This creates days that feel exhausting without feeling productive. You worked hard, stayed busy, handled everything—and still feel like nothing real got done. That's because real work requires sustained attention, and sustained attention's become rare.

How to Apply This Today

For the next task you do—doesn't matter what—give it complete attention for its entire duration. No phone nearby. No other tabs open. No "I'll just check this one thing quickly." Complete attention, start to finish, for one task.

You'll be shocked by two things. First, how much faster the work goes when you're not constantly restarting after interruptions. Second, how difficult it is to maintain that attention without your mind reaching for something else to check. That difficulty? That's how much your attention's been trained to scatter. That's where your time's actually going—not into the work, but into the gaps between fragments of focus.

"Time's most often lost when it's borrowed from what matters."

Tempus alienum saepe subripit quod suum esse debebat.

What Seneca Meant

Time isn't only wasted on obvious trivialities—scrolling, procrastinating, genuinely pointless things. That waste is visible, easy to name, relatively easy to address. What Seneca's pointing to is more subtle and more damaging: time taken from what deserves it and given to what doesn't.

Borrowing sounds temporary. You'll get to the important thing later, you'll make it up, you'll find time somewhere else. Meanwhile, you handle the quick task, respond to the urgent message, deal with what just came up. The borrowing feels harmless, feels necessary even—this will just take a minute, then I'll get to what matters. But when repeated, borrowing quietly reshapes priorities. What matters most gets postponed in favor of what's easier, quicker, more immediately satisfying. Over time, important intentions become permanently undernourished while trivial demands get fed constantly.

Why This Still Matters

Most people protect time in general but not specific uses of it. They say family matters, then work through dinner. They value deep work, then interrupt it to answer quick questions. Individual instances feel reasonable. This really will just take a minute. But the pattern, repeated daily, creates a life where important things are always second in line.

How to Apply This Today

Track this for one day. Notice which commitments consistently get shortened, interrupted, or postponed to make room for other things. Pay attention to the direction of borrowing. What takes from what? If important things routinely get shortened to accommodate urgent demands, you're not managing time—you're letting urgency steal from importance.

"Nothing we lose is more difficult to recover than time."

Nullum bonum tam difficulter recipitur quam tempus.

What Seneca Meant

Irreversibility. Other losses allow compensation. Money can be re-earned. Relationships repaired. Opportunities circle back. Time? Once spent, it's gone.

Why This Still Matters

Modern life encourages treating time as flexible, as something that can be made up later, borrowed against, shuffled around. "I'll get to that next week." "We'll spend time together after this busy period." "I'll focus on what matters once things calm down." This framing assumes time's renewable, that missed opportunities will return, that postponed attention can be recovered.

But it can't. The particular conditions that made something possible—the age your kids are right now, the energy you have this year, the relationships that exist in their current form—those conditions are temporary. Time doesn't just march forward; it closes possibilities behind it as it goes. What you could have done yesterday you might not be able to do tomorrow.

This finality should make time the resource people guard most carefully. Instead, it's the one they spend most carelessly. Why? Because the loss doesn't hurt immediately. Miss a workout and you feel it. Waste money and you see the account balance drop. But waste an hour, a day, a year? The cost doesn't register until later—often much later—when you look back and realize how much slipped away while you were planning to start paying attention.

How to Apply This Today

Start thinking of time as closing behind you, not opening ahead. That shift—subtle as it sounds—changes how you weigh the next hour. It's not a resource you'll have more of tomorrow. It's a resource that's diminishing right now, this moment, while you're reading this sentence. Ask yourself: if this hour, this day, this year couldn't be recovered or repeated, would I spend it differently?

"Your time reveals your life more clearly than your intentions."

Qualis vita, talis dies.

What Seneca Meant

Intentions describe what you hope to do, what you value, what you tell yourself matters. Time shows what actually happened, where attention actually went, what actually got prioritized when you had to choose. Often there's a gap between what someone says matters and where their time consistently goes.

Why This Still Matters

It's easy to hold clear intentions while living days that contradict them. You value health but skip workouts. You prioritize family but work late constantly. You want meaningful work but spend hours on email. The mismatch goes unnoticed because intention feels sincere and days feel necessary. But sincere intention without corresponding behavior is just wishful thinking.

How to Apply This Today

Look at last week as if it belonged to someone else. Don't bring your knowledge of all the reasons things happened the way they did, all the context that makes everything feel necessary and justified. Just look at the calendar: where did the time go?

What would you conclude about this person's priorities based solely on that evidence? If the answer doesn't match what you'd say your priorities are, that gap is the problem. Not the intentions—those are easy. The problem is the distance between what you claim matters and what gets your time when time's actually being spent. Close that gap or admit your stated priorities aren't your actual priorities. The calendar doesn't lie.

Chapter 4

Living as If Time Matters

Time's often acknowledged only after it's been lost. In daily life, it's treated as background—something assumed, rarely examined, easily postponed. Yet how time's used reveals priorities more clearly than stated intentions.

Seneca shifts attention from loss to use. After noticing where time goes, he asks how it's held. Living as if time matters doesn't require urgency or constant focus. It requires clarity about what deserves presence and what can be left aside without regret.

Much of what delays action feels reasonable. Conditions are expected to improve. Obligations appear temporary. Attention's deferred in the name of preparation or responsibility. Seneca examines these habits closely, not to condemn them, but to test whether they serve what matters or quietly replace it.

He's attentive to deferred living—the tendency to treat meaningful action as something that belongs to a later phase. This postponement rarely announces itself as avoidance. It appears as patience, planning, or caution. Over time, it reshapes life around waiting rather than engagement.

The reflections that follow consider what it means to act without haste while remaining present. They focus on attention, priority, and proportion. Living as if time matters begins there, not with intensity, but with steadiness.

"We treat time as abundant, even while spending it as if it were endless."

Tamquam in perpetuum victuri vivimus.

What Seneca Meant

A quiet contradiction sits at the center of daily life. People behave as though time will always be available, even while using it without any restraint whatsoever. Decisions get postponed. Attention disperses across dozens of minor demands. Priorities get delayed under the assumption there'll be another opportunity—tomorrow, next week, someday when things calm down.

The gap between how time's spoken about and how it's actually handled creates the problem. Everyone agrees time's precious. Everyone nods when someone says life's short. Then everyone goes back to treating today as rehearsal for some future moment when they'll finally start paying attention. Habits form without review. Loss feels abstract until it becomes final.

Why This Still Matters

Modern life reinforces this strange assumption at every turn. Plans get deferred. Commitments stretch indefinitely. Attention's borrowed from the present in favor of future readiness that never quite arrives. Time's acknowledged as valuable in theory, yet treated as flexible in practice—something that can be made up later, rearranged, shuffled around without consequence.

How to Apply This Today

Look at your calendar for today. Not tomorrow's plans or next week's intentions—today's actual hours. How many were claimed deliberately? How many just filled themselves according to whoever asked loudest? The difference between treating time as available and treating it as already claimed shows up in those small choices, made or avoided, throughout a single ordinary day.

"What we delay is often what we say matters most."

Optima quaeque differimus.

What Seneca Meant

Watch what actually gets postponed. It's never the trivial stuff. Answering routine emails? That happens immediately. Checking notifications? Instant. But the hard conversation with someone who matters? Postponed. The project that requires real thought? Delayed. The decision that takes courage? Pushed to next week, then next month, then someday when conditions feel right.

Delay rarely affects things that don't matter. It targets precisely what requires commitment, effort, or attention. This happens because deferring what matters most protects us from discomfort while letting us believe we're being prudent, careful, responsible. Over time, the pattern reshapes life around avoidance disguised as planning.

Why This Still Matters

Most people feel responsible and careful while consistently deferring what would actually give their life coherence. Important conversations stay perpetually "upcoming." Meaningful work gets scheduled for when there's more time. Personal commitments get placed just beyond reach—not refused, just postponed until conditions improve.

Delay becomes normalized, even respected, while genuine engagement gets postponed indefinitely. The calendar fills with urgent demands. What matters waits.

How to Apply This Today

Pull up your task list or mental inventory of what needs doing. Divide it into two columns: what you've been postponing and what you've been handling immediately. Look at the gap between those lists. That gap? That's your actual priorities, not the ones you claim.

"Living later is a habit formed one day at a time."

Dum expectamus, vita transcurrit.

What Seneca Meant

Postponed living accumulates through small, reasonable-seeming choices. Each individual delay makes sense in isolation. This particular conversation can wait. This project can start next month. This decision doesn't need to happen today.

Why This Still Matters

Life's often structured around undefined future phases. After work stabilizes. After responsibilities ease. After conditions improve. After things finally calm down. These phases remain permanently out of reach because they're not actual conditions but excuses dressed up as planning.

Meanwhile, the present becomes a holding area. You're managing, maintaining, getting through—but not really living, not fully engaged, not doing the things you tell yourself you'll get to later. Later becomes where all your real intentions live, and it stays forever just beyond your current circumstances. The habit forms gradually, without resistance, because it rarely presents itself as avoidance. It feels like being sensible.

How to Apply This Today

List three things you've postponed until "things calm down." Now answer honestly: in the last five years, have things ever actually calmed down? If the answer's no, you're not waiting for the right time. You're avoiding what matters behind reasonable-sounding conditions that'll never be met. The right time is now, with the constraints you have, or it's never.

"Life becomes thinner when attention's always postponed."

Vita in expectatione consumitur.

What Seneca Meant

Attention's the substance of living. When it's consistently deferred—reserved for some future moment assumed to be more suitable—life narrows without any single dramatic loss. There's no catastrophe, no obvious failure, just a gradual thinning. What matters isn't removed outright; it's diluted by delay until it barely registers.

Why This Still Matters

Many days get spent preparing for later engagement. Focus gets reserved for tomorrow. Presence gets postponed to next week. Energy's saved for when conditions improve. Over time, this creates a paradox: circumstances appear full—busy schedule, constant demands, lots happening—yet the present feels undernourished, thin, somehow incomplete despite all the activity.

The thinning's subtle. You're not doing nothing. You're just perpetually getting ready instead of being engaged, always one step away from actually beginning whatever it is you're preparing for.

How to Apply This Today

Notice when attention gets habitually postponed rather than withheld by genuine necessity. That conversation you keep planning to have "when there's more time"—have it today. That project you're endlessly preparing for—start it this afternoon. Small acts of presence often restore more substance than elaborate plans for future engagement ever could.

"To live well requires deciding what deserves your time."

Non est vivere, sed valere vita.

What Seneca Meant

Living well functions as selection, not accumulation. Time gains shape when judgment determines where it belongs. Without deliberate choice about what deserves attention, time simply fills according to availability, urgency, or habit.

The difference between a directed life and a drifting one often comes down to this: whether time's allocated by decision or by default. Default means whatever arrives next gets attention. Decision means judgment determines what's worth the resource.

Why This Still Matters

Choice gets replaced by availability in most modern schedules. What appears next receives attention automatically. Whoever asks loudest gets priority. Whatever feels urgent commands focus. This creates movement without coherence—lots happening, lots handled, yet important priorities remain dependent on chance rather than judgment.

Days fill completely without anything that truly matters getting sustained attention. Not because there's no time, but because time's never claimed deliberately. It's assigned by urgency, doled out to whatever demands it most insistently.

How to Apply This Today

Before this day ends, answer one question: did anything that happened today serve what you'd say you care about most? Not what felt urgent, not what someone else needed, not what maintained the status quo—what you'd claim matters if someone asked directly. If the answer's no, tomorrow presents another chance to let judgment guide time instead of letting time fill itself.

"Presence is lost when everything is treated as preparation."

Dum parat, vivit nemo.

What Seneca Meant

Preparation can displace living entirely. Readiness becomes a permanent state. Action gets delayed in its name, indefinitely.

Why This Still Matters

Many lives are structured as endless sequences of preparation—planning, organizing, optimizing, getting ready, building capacity, creating conditions. These activities feel responsible, productive, even virtuous. Yet when they dominate, they leave almost no room for the experience they're supposedly preparing for.

You're always getting ready to begin, always one step away from starting, always waiting for conditions to be ideal before fully engaging. The preparation itself becomes the activity, while what it's meant to prepare for gets postponed to some future moment that never quite arrives because preparation never feels complete.

This creates a strange inversion: life becomes about getting ready to live rather than actually living. The present's consumed by preparation for a future that stays perpetually out of reach.

How to Apply This Today

Count how many times this month you refined the plan instead of starting. If it's more than twice, you're not preparing—you're avoiding. Preparation has value when it's bounded, when it leads somewhere. Endless refinement, perpetual optimization, constant reorganization? That's avoidance wearing the mask of diligence.

"Time matters most when it's treated as something to be used, not saved."

Tempus non servandum est, sed utendum.

What Seneca Meant

The focus here isn't urgency—it's engagement. Time gains meaning through use. When it's merely conserved, protected, held onto indefinitely without application, it remains abstract. Unused time doesn't accumulate value like unused money in an account. It just passes, unclaimed and wasted through preservation itself.

This sounds counterintuitive because we're trained to think saving is wise. With money, it often is. With time, saving typically means postponing—protecting hours and days for some undefined future use that never materializes because the right moment never arrives.

Why This Still Matters

Many people protect time in theory while hesitating to commit it where it counts. Important decisions get delayed "until there's time to think clearly." Meaningful projects wait "until the schedule clears." Significant conversations get postponed "until we can really focus." What's being protected never gets used. It just passes, saved in theory but lost in practice.

How to Apply This Today

Identify where you're protecting time instead of applying it. That hour you're saving for when you're less tired? Use it now. That conversation you're postponing until you have time to do it right? Have it today, imperfectly. Use clarifies value in ways preservation never does. Time spent badly teaches more than time saved indefinitely.

"Waiting for the right moment often replaces the moment itself."

Dum idoneum tempus exspectamus, praeterit.

What Seneca Meant

Waiting functions as substitution. The search for ideal timing quietly displaces action entirely. What gets postponed feels sensible, even careful—you're not refusing to act, just waiting for better conditions. Meanwhile, the moment that was meant to be improved passes unclaimed. The waiting itself becomes the activity, replacing what it was supposed to enable.

Why This Still Matters

The expectation of perfect conditions is everywhere. Readiness becomes a requirement that's rarely met. You'll start the project when work calms down. You'll have the conversation when emotions aren't running high. You'll make the decision when you have all the information. Life continues while attention remains fixed on a future moment that never fully arrives, because something's always slightly off, slightly imperfect, slightly not-yet-ready.

How to Apply This Today

Look at what you're currently waiting for better conditions to do. Ask directly: what specifically needs to improve before you begin? If you can't name concrete conditions, you're not waiting for the right moment—you're avoiding action behind the language of prudence. The moment you're waiting for is probably already here, just imperfect, like every actual moment always is.

"Time shows its value when it's chosen deliberately."

Tempus indicat pretium suum cum eligitur.

What Seneca Meant

Choice reveals value. Time makes priorities visible through selection rather than through intention or declaration.

Why This Still Matters

Intentions remain sincere yet unrealized constantly. "I value family time." "I prioritize health." "I care about meaningful work." These statements feel true when said.

But days fill according to demand rather than decision, and the gap between stated values and actual time allocation grows wider without anyone noticing.

Time chosen deliberately makes priorities visible without requiring explanation or justification. What gets hours of attention? What gets minutes? What gets consistently postponed? The pattern reveals what actually matters, regardless of what's claimed.

Without deliberate choice, time reflects pressure more than value, urgency more than importance, availability more than priority.

How to Apply This Today

Track one thing today: was your time chosen or assigned? Did you decide where attention went, or did demands decide for you? Even one deliberately chosen hour—protected, claimed, used for something that matters rather than something that shouted—shifts the day's weight from reactive to directed.

"Time gains weight when it's lived with attention."

Tempus gravitatem capit cum attenditur.

What Seneca Meant

Attention gives time substance. The same span—same minutes on the clock, same hours in the day—can feel empty or full depending on how closely it's held. Presence alters experience. Time lived with attention has weight, density, texture. Time passed without attention feels thin, forgettable, gone without having registered as lived.

Why This Still Matters

Many days feel thin despite being objectively full. Schedules overflow. Tasks get completed. Hours pass quickly. Yet the day leaves almost no trace, no sense of substance, no feeling of having actually been present for your own life. This happens when attention divides, scatters, or disperses across too many things at once. Presence weakens. Time accumulates without depth.

How to Apply This Today

For one task today—doesn't matter which—give it your complete attention. No background checking. No mental sidebar conversations. No splitting focus between this and planning the next thing. Complete attention for its entire duration. You'll notice two things: how much fuller that time feels compared to fragmented hours, and how hard it is to maintain that attention without your mind reaching for something else. That difficulty shows how habitual fragmentation's become, and that fullness shows what's lost every time attention divides.

"A life feels coherent when time's used in line with what matters."

Vita congruit cum tempus consentit.

What Seneca Meant

Coherence emerges from alignment, not achievement. When daily time use matches underlying values—not perfectly, but recognizably—life holds its shape without constant effort or justification. There's no gap between what you claim matters and where your hours actually go. Days don't require explanation because they speak for themselves.

Why This Still Matters

Most people experience persistent tension between stated values and actual time allocation. This tension rarely comes from lack of intention. You genuinely do value what you say you value. The problem's the gap between value and time, between what matters in theory and what gets hours in practice.

That misalignment creates a low-grade unease that follows you through otherwise successful days. You're handling everything, meeting obligations, staying busy—and still feeling like you're missing what's actually important. The feeling comes from incoherence, from time and value pulling in different directions without anyone acknowledging the split.

How to Apply This Today

Compare two lists: what you'd say matters most if asked directly, and where your time actually went this week. The gap between those lists? That's where the incoherence lives. You don't have to close it completely or immediately. Just see it clearly. Coherence starts with honest recognition of where alignment exists and where it's been lost.

PART III

EMOTION:
ANGER, FEAR, AND
SELF-COMMAND

Chapter 5

Understanding Anger Before It Takes Over

Anger often arrives with speed. It feels immediate, justified, directed outward. Attention narrows, response follows quickly. By the time anger's fully visible, it's already shaped judgment.

Seneca examines anger at its earliest stages. His interest lies in how a reaction begins, not in how it ends. He traces anger to interpretation—how events are assessed, meanings assigned, expectations formed. What matters most is the moment when judgment starts to harden.

Small signals appear early. Irritation during delay. Resistance to interruption. A sense of being wronged before harm's clear. These moments pass quickly, but they carry direction. Seneca treats them as points of choice, where attention can still influence outcome.

Anger grows when it's allowed to build momentum. Once it accelerates, proportion's lost and response becomes difficult to adjust. Seneca's focus remains on prevention through awareness rather than control through force. He returns repeatedly to the value of pause, not as suppression, but as space for judgment to remain present.

The reflections that follow explore anger as a process rather than an event. Each quote isolates a stage where escalation becomes possible. Together, they clarify how restraint begins before anger feels strong, and how dignity's preserved through early attention.

"Anger begins the moment judgment hardens."

Ira ex iudicio nascitur.

What Seneca Meant

Anger doesn't start with the event—it starts with how you decide the event means. A situation occurs. Your mind interprets it. Meaning gets assigned. Certainty forms quickly, often before the facts are even clear. Once that interpretation settles into conviction, emotion follows automatically.

The anger you feel isn't the product of what happened. It's the product of how your mind decided to read what happened. Someone's late? Your mind decides it's disrespect. A project gets delayed? Your mind decides it's sabotage. A comment lands wrong? Your mind decides it's an attack. The emotion that follows feels immediate, spontaneous, inevitable—but it's been prepared by an interpretation that happened so fast you barely noticed it forming.

Why This Still Matters

Most reactions feel like they just appear, fully formed, triggered directly by circumstances. The sense that "this made me angry" feels true because the gap between event and emotion is so brief. But there's always an interpretation between stimulus and response, and that interpretation's where anger actually begins.

When evaluation happens too quickly, when judgment hardens before consideration, response narrows. Options disappear. The path from event to anger feels automatic because the interpretive step happened too fast to register.

How to Apply This Today

Next time you feel anger starting, stop before it speaks. Just for three seconds. In that gap, ask: "How am I reading this situation right now?" Not whether your reading's correct—just what it is. Anger often loses force the moment you see the interpretation that created it. Making that interpretation visible, even briefly, often reveals how much of the anger formed before the facts were settled.

"We feel wronged before we know whether harm has occurred."

Ante iniuriam nos ipsos laedimus.

What Seneca Meant

The feeling of being wronged arrives before evidence confirms harm. Someone doesn't respond to your message—within minutes, you're offended. A colleague takes credit in a meeting—immediately, you feel undermined. Your expectation of how things should go fills the gap where facts should be, and anger gains force not from what actually happened but from what you assumed was happening.

Why This Still Matters

Conflicts escalate because meaning gets assigned too quickly. A delay, a tone, an interruption—these get read as intent before context arrives. Once offense is presumed, response follows automatically, even when the situation's still ambiguous.

Someone's quiet in a conversation? Must be angry at you. A text comes back shorter than usual? They're pulling away. A decision gets made without your input? You've been dismissed. The story writes itself before reality has a chance to clarify what's actually happening, and by the time facts arrive, you've already responded to the story you told yourself.

How to Apply This Today

Pause between event and interpretation. That pause doesn't need to be long—thirty seconds is often enough. When irritation spikes before clarity, ask one question: "What else could this mean?" Not to excuse genuinely harmful behavior, but to prevent anger from forming around assumptions that haven't been tested. Most conflicts that could have been avoided started exactly here: feeling wronged before harm was confirmed.

"The earliest signs of anger are small and easily ignored."

Ira in parvis incipit.

What Seneca Meant

Anger doesn't arrive fully formed. It begins with irritation, resistance, a slight tightening of attention.

Why This Still Matters

Escalation rarely begins with intensity. It begins with tolerance of small reactions that feel justified in the moment. Someone interrupts you—minor irritation, easy to dismiss. They do it again—resistance builds, still manageable. By the third time, the reaction's disproportionate, and you can't understand why you're so angry about something so small.

The problem isn't the third interruption. It's that the first two registered just enough to set direction without registering enough to trigger awareness. Those small moments accumulate silently, and by the time anger feels strong enough to notice, it's already moving with momentum.

These signals feel minor, and that's precisely why they pass unexamined. Yet they indicate direction. When ignored, they allow anger to grow without resistance, building strength in the background until it surfaces with force that seems to come from nowhere.

How to Apply This Today

Track the earliest signals of irritation today. Not the big moments—the small ones. The slight edge in someone's voice that makes your shoulders tense. The minor delay that creates a flash of impatience. These moments carry more influence than later attempts to regain control, because they're where direction gets set. Noticing them early—when they're still small—is where restraint actually begins.

"Once anger gathers speed, judgment loses proportion."

Crescente ira, ratio deficit.

What Seneca Meant

Momentum changes how judgment operates. Once anger begins moving quickly, perspective narrows. Alternatives disappear. Response feels necessary rather than chosen. Proportion's lost not because reason vanishes entirely, but because it gets overtaken by emotional momentum that's already accelerating.

Why This Still Matters

Anger often feels strongest when it's already moving. At that stage, response becomes difficult to adjust. You're not choosing what to say—the anger's choosing it, and you're following. Decisions made under that kind of momentum tend to feel completely justified in the moment and deeply regrettable afterward, once the momentum fades and proportion returns.

How to Apply This Today

When reactions begin speeding up—when you're thinking of three responses before finishing the first one, when your heart rate's climbing, when silence starts feeling impossible to maintain—that's momentum signaling that judgment's no longer fully present. The intervention isn't forcing calm. It's just slowing the response rate enough for judgment to catch up to emotion.

"Anger persuades us that acting immediately is strength."

Ira se celeritatem virtutem esse persuadet.

What Seneca Meant

Anger functions as persuasion. It presents speed as decisiveness. Immediate reaction as courage. Delay as weakness. This framing distorts judgment at the moment when clarity matters most. Haste replaces evaluation, impulse gets mistaken for resolve, and action taken under anger's influence feels powerful precisely because it skips the hesitation that comes from actually thinking.

The persuasion's subtle because it arrives wrapped in something that feels like strength. "Don't let them get away with this." "Say what needs to be said." "Show them you won't be pushed around." The internal voice sounds confident, urgent, necessary. But that voice isn't strength—it's anger doing what anger does, creating urgency to bypass judgment.

Why This Still Matters

Many responses feel necessary simply because they arrive with force. The pressure to act quickly narrows options and silences reflection before it can surface. What feels powerful in the moment—the sharp reply, the immediate escalation, the refusal to wait—often reduces choice and limits what becomes possible afterward.

How to Apply This Today

Next time replying immediately feels urgent—whether it's a confrontational message, a public disagreement, or a tense exchange that demands response right now—ask one question before responding: "Will waiting five minutes make this worse?" If the answer's no, wait. That brief delay often restores proportion without diminishing your actual authority. Strength that requires speed to feel real usually isn't strength. It's anger disguised as decisiveness.

"When anger speaks first, reason follows late."

Ira loquitur, ratio sequitur.

What Seneca Meant

Sequence matters. When anger leads, reason gets forced into justification rather than guidance. Words get chosen, actions get taken, explanation comes afterward. Judgment no longer directs response—it defends what anger already said.

This reversal happens so quickly it's almost invisible. Anger speaks. The words land. Then reason arrives to explain why those words made sense, why the reaction was justified, why anyone in that situation would have responded the same way. But that's post-hoc rationalization, not actual reasoning. Real judgment guides action. This version just defends what already happened.

Why This Still Matters

Conflicts deepen because explanation replaces evaluation. Once words are spoken in anger, repair becomes harder. The damage isn't just in what was said—it's in the fact that reason arrived too late to shape the moment, leaving only cleanup where guidance should have been.

How to Apply This Today

Before speaking in a charged moment, answer this: which voice is forming the words right now? If it's anger—if the response feels urgent, if the tone's already sharp, if you're building momentum toward something that'll feel good to say—wait. Just until judgment can speak first instead of arriving late to defend what anger already did.

"Delay is the first proof of strength in anger."

Maximum irae remedium mora est.

What Seneca Meant

Delay functions as judgment, not hesitation.

Why This Still Matters

Anger frames delay as weakness. Immediate reaction feels decisive, powerful, necessary. Yet responses made in haste typically narrow options and increase cost. What feels like strength—the instant reply, the quick escalation, the refusal to pause—usually just hands control to impulse.

Delay doesn't mean suppressing anger or pretending it doesn't exist. It means preventing anger from setting the terms of response. The pause interrupts momentum and restores space where choice can operate again. In that space, judgment returns. Not perfectly, not completely, but enough to widen options beyond what anger alone would choose.

Delay preserves range and keeps authority intact. The response you give after waiting isn't weaker for having waited—it's stronger because it reflects choice rather than momentum.

How to Apply This Today

Notice how even brief pauses change the quality of response. Five minutes between provocation and reply. Thirty seconds between impulse and action. That gap—small as it is—creates room for judgment to return. Time doesn't eliminate anger, but it does create distance between feeling it and acting from it. That distance is where restraint actually lives.

"Restraint preserves authority more than retaliation."

Retinere iram maius est quam ulcisci.

What Seneca Meant

Authority comes from command over yourself, not others. Retaliation hands control to anger. Restraint keeps judgment in charge and response aligned with intention. The moment anger dictates action, authority erodes—not because the grievance isn't real, but because the response demonstrates loss of command rather than possession of it.

Why This Still Matters

Many situations reward composure more than force. Loss of restraint often weakens credibility, even when the grievance feels completely justified. When you retaliate in anger, what people remember isn't whether you were right—it's that you lost control. Authority erodes when anger dictates action, because authority fundamentally means being in command of yourself first.

How to Apply This Today

In situations where silence or measured response carries more weight than confrontation—choosing not to escalate a tense exchange at work, for instance, or responding to provocation with composure rather than matching energy—the restraint itself communicates authority. It shows that reaction's a choice, not a reflex. Proving a point through retaliation might feel satisfying momentarily, but preserving influence through restraint often accomplishes more over time.

"Anger fades when judgment is reclaimed."

Ira deficit ubi iudicium redit.

What Seneca Meant

Anger doesn't need to be suppressed, expelled, or wrestled into submission. It weakens naturally when judgment resumes its role. Once interpretation gets reconsidered and proportion restored, anger loses its force without requiring direct confrontation.

This happens because anger depends on a particular way of seeing the situation—a narrowed perspective that emphasizes offense, urgency, or threat. When that perspective broadens, when other interpretations become visible again, the emotional state shifts on its own. You don't fight the anger. You adjust the understanding that's maintaining it.

Why This Still Matters

Many people attempt to manage anger through effort alone—trying to calm down, suppress the feeling, force composure. What actually changes the state is a shift in understanding. When judgment broadens, emotion follows. The anger that felt overwhelming when you were convinced someone betrayed you often dissolves when you learn they had reasons you hadn't considered.

How to Apply This Today

Focus on reclaiming perspective rather than controlling feeling. Ask: "What am I not seeing right now?" Not to excuse harmful behavior or invalidate your reaction, but to check whether your current understanding of the situation is complete. Clear judgment often dissolves anger without confrontation, simply by restoring proportion to a perspective that had narrowed too far.

"Anger costs authority before it brings relief."

Ira imperium amittit.

What Seneca Meant

Loss of command happens first. Relief, if it comes at all, comes second—but by then the cost's already been paid. Anger presents itself as a way to assert strength, defend position, or refuse to be pushed around. In practice, it frequently weakens credibility and limits influence.

Once authority's surrendered to impulse, repairing that loss requires far more effort than restraint would have cost in the first place. You might feel better after expressing anger—tension released, words finally said. But what you've lost is harder to recover than what you've gained. The relief is momentary. The loss of authority persists.

The trade happens quickly and often without awareness. Anger promises power in the moment, delivers relief through expression, and quietly extracts authority as payment. What's lost first isn't calm—it's direction. Judgment gets forced into a secondary role, and reason arrives late to defend what impulse already chose.

Why This Still Matters

When credibility erodes, influence shrinks. Even when the grievance was genuine, even when the anger felt completely justified, the response determines what happens next. Authority depends on being in command of yourself first, and that command becomes visible through restraint, not release.

How to Apply This Today

Before anger speaks, ask: "Is this being used to regain control, or is it quietly giving control away?" The honest answer to that question often changes what happens next. If anger's about reasserting authority, it's probably doing the opposite. Real authority doesn't need anger to establish itself—it shows up through measured response that reflects judgment, not impulse.

Chapter 6

Responding Without Escalation

After anger's been recognized and slowed, another question follows: how to respond without making the situation heavier. Seneca's attention shifts from inner reaction to outward action. What matters here isn't the absence of feeling, but the quality of response that follows it.

Every response carries consequence. Words spoken, decisions made, tone chosen—all shape what comes next. Seneca examines this moment closely because it's where dignity's either preserved or surrendered. Once escalation begins, choice narrows and authority weakens.

He treats restraint as an active capacity. Holding back isn't passivity. It's a form of command that keeps judgment present while pressure pushes toward reaction. Delay, silence, or measured speech function as tools that protect range rather than limit it.

Seneca's attentive to situations where escalation feels justified. Insult, provocation, disrespect—all invite response. Yet he consistently returns to proportion. A response that matches the size of the moment preserves clarity. One that exceeds it creates consequences that outlast the original cause.

The reflections that follow explore how restraint operates in practice. They focus on timing, choice, and the preservation of authority under strain. Responding without escalation's treated as a discipline of judgment, exercised quietly in moments that often pass unnoticed.

"The response shapes the outcome more than the offense."

Plus nocet responsio quam iniuria.

What Seneca Meant

What follows an offense carries more weight than the offense itself. Response determines direction. The original provocation might have been minor, forgettable, containable—but how you answer it decides whether the moment passes or expands. A measured reply contains the situation. An excessive one amplifies it, giving energy to something that could've dissolved on its own.

The offense happens, then ends. Your response creates what comes next. The original cause becomes less important than how judgment chooses to act upon it. Someone says something careless—that's one moment. How you respond becomes ten moments, each with its own consequences.

Why This Still Matters

Situations worsen through reaction more often than through cause. A sharp reply, a raised voice, a public escalation—any of these can turn brief tension into lasting problem. What people remember isn't usually the initial offense. They remember your response to it, how you handled pressure, whether you maintained composure or lost it.

How to Apply This Today

Before responding to something that bothers you, ask one question: "Will this response reduce the situation or extend it?" The answer's usually clear if you're honest. Outcome gets decided at that point, in the gap between provocation and reply. Most conflicts that could've ended quietly instead grow because the response exceeded what the moment required.

"Escalation begins when response seeks victory rather than proportion."

Contentio oritur cum vincere volumus.

What Seneca Meant

Motive shapes outcome. Escalation follows when response aims to win rather than to resolve, to dominate rather than to clarify. Judgment becomes competitive. The question shifts from "What does this situation need?" to "Who's going to prevail here?" Once that shift occurs, the response no longer serves clarity—it serves assertion, pride, the need to be right or to be seen winning.

Why This Still Matters

Exchanges turn adversarial quickly. The desire to be right, to prevail, to defend status overtakes attention. Resolution recedes as position takes center stage. You're no longer trying to address the actual issue—you're trying to establish dominance, prove a point, make sure everyone knows you won't be pushed around.

This happens in meetings, in relationships, in any situation where status feels threatened. Someone challenges your position, and instantly the goal shifts from finding the best answer to defending your original stance. The issue becomes secondary. Winning becomes primary. And escalation follows automatically because winning requires force, assertion, making your voice louder than theirs.

How to Apply This Today

Notice when your reply's being shaped to assert standing rather than address the issue. For example: choosing tone or words to appear strong in front of others rather than to keep the situation contained. That shift—from resolution to victory—is where escalation becomes inevitable. Catching it early, before response is formed, often prevents unnecessary conflict.

"Measured response keeps authority intact."

Modus servat imperium.

What Seneca Meant

Authority's maintained when response reflects judgment rather than impulse. Measure signals command—it shows that reaction's been considered and chosen, not released under pressure.

Why This Still Matters

Credibility depends less on force than on steadiness. A controlled response communicates reliability and keeps options open. Authority weakens when reaction appears automatic, when it's clear that circumstances dictated your behavior rather than judgment guiding it.

Think about people whose authority you respect. It's rarely the ones who react loudly or immediately. It's the ones who pause, consider, then respond in proportion to what the situation actually requires. Their measured approach communicates something that force never does: they're in command of themselves first, which means they can be trusted with command over other things.

How to Apply This Today

Before any charged response, ask: "Does this reflect choice or momentum?" If it's momentum—if the reply's forming automatically, if you're reacting without pause—wait. Even thirty seconds changes what you're capable of choosing. Authority follows the former, not the latter. Measure preserves it. Reaction surrenders it.

"Silence can hold more authority than immediate reply."

Taciturnitas saepe plus potest.

What Seneca Meant

Restraint functions as presence, not absence. Silence isn't empty space—it's active choice. By withholding response, judgment stays in command. Silence prevents momentum from dictating action and keeps the situation from expanding beyond its original scope.

This isn't avoidance. It's control. The person who can remain silent when provoked demonstrates authority more clearly than the person who has to respond immediately. Because silence requires holding tension without releasing it, maintaining composure while pressure builds, staying present to the moment without needing to fill it with reaction.

Why This Still Matters

Many exchanges feel pressured by immediacy. The expectation to answer quickly creates stress and invites misjudgment. Silence, used deliberately, often stabilizes situations that would otherwise intensify. It creates space for emotion to settle, for facts to clarify, for better options to become visible.

Not every moment requires response to remain intact. Most situations don't need your immediate input. They just want it—there's a difference. Silence preserves your ability to choose when and how to engage, rather than letting urgency decide for you.

How to Apply This Today

Practice silence in one low-stakes situation today. Someone says something that would normally trigger immediate reply—a criticism, a challenge, a question that feels loaded. Instead of responding right away, stay quiet for fifteen seconds. Just fifteen. Notice what changes in that gap. Often, the compulsion to respond dissolves, or a better response becomes clear, or the other person fills the silence with information that changes how you'd answer.

"Timing determines whether a response calms or inflames."

Tempus responsionis facit discrimen.

What Seneca Meant

The same words produce different effects depending on when they're delivered. Timing shapes reception. A response offered too soon often amplifies emotion, while one given later allows proportion to return. This isn't about delay for delay's sake—it's about recognizing that words land differently depending on the state of the person receiving them.

Why This Still Matters

Pressure to respond immediately is everywhere. Yet early responses typically carry residual emotion—yours and theirs. That emotional charge distorts how words are heard. What you intend as clarification gets received as attack. What you mean as boundary-setting gets heard as aggression. The content might be right, but the timing makes it wrong.

Delay changes the conditions under which words are received and understood. The same explanation that would've sparked an argument at 9 PM might be calmly received at 9 AM. Not because the words changed, but because the emotional context shifted.

How to Apply This Today

When tension's high, ask: "Is now the right time for this to land well?" Not "Do I have good points to make"—you probably do. But will those points be heard the way you intend them, or will timing guarantee they're received badly? Waiting often transforms a message that would've escalated the situation into one that actually resolves it.

"Escalation feeds on speed more than substance."

Celeritas contentionem alit.

What Seneca Meant

Speed accelerates reaction and reduces judgment. Substance becomes secondary as response rushes ahead of evaluation. Escalation thrives when tempo replaces thought, when the gap between stimulus and response disappears entirely.

Fast exchanges intensify conflict even when issues are minor. Speed amplifies reaction and compresses understanding. Each reply comes quicker than the last, building momentum that makes restraint progressively harder to recover. Before long, you're not responding to what's actually being said—you're responding to your own reaction to their reaction to your reaction.

Why This Still Matters

Modern communication accelerates everything. Instant messaging, real-time threads, the expectation of immediate response—all these compress the space where judgment operates. Speed feels like engagement, like being responsive and present. But speed often just means reacting before you've understood what you're reacting to.

How to Apply This Today

When exchanges start speeding up—when replies get shorter, when the pace quickens, when you're formulating responses before the other person's finished speaking—that's the moment to deliberately slow down. Not permanently. Just interrupt the tempo. Take an extra ten seconds before replying. Let one message sit unanswered for an hour instead of thirty seconds. Slowing pace often restores clarity without requiring effort. The substance doesn't change. The speed does, and that's often enough.

"A measured response preserves range."

Modus spatium servat.

What Seneca Meant

Restraint keeps options open. When response is measured, future choices remain available. Escalation narrows range by committing judgment too quickly, forcing outcomes before alternatives have been explored. Measure protects flexibility and keeps consequence proportionate to the actual situation rather than to the emotional intensity of the moment.

Why This Still Matters

Situations become fixed because response closes doors early. Strong reactions limit alternatives and force outcomes. You say something in anger that can't be unsaid. You make a public statement that commits you to a position. You escalate to a level that makes de-escalation difficult without appearing weak. Each of these narrows what's possible afterward.

Preserving range often matters more than resolving the moment decisively. Quick resolution feels satisfying, but it often sacrifices better options that would've emerged with slightly more patience. Measured response keeps those options alive.

How to Apply This Today

Before responding to something charged, ask: "Does this response expand or contract what can happen next?" If it contracts—if it forces a particular outcome, commits you publicly, or makes certain paths impossible—consider whether that closure is necessary right now. Range is often preserved simply by not committing fully until you have to.

"Dignity's maintained when response doesn't mirror provocation."

Dignitas servatur cum provocatio non imitatur.

What Seneca Meant

When response mirrors provocation, escalation becomes symmetrical and self-reinforcing. Someone speaks sharply, so you speak sharply back. They raise their voice, so you raise yours. They attack, so you counterattack. The mirroring feels fair, feels like balance, feels like you're not letting them get away with anything.

But dignity comes from asymmetry—from choosing a response that reflects judgment rather than stimulus. Breaking the pattern, refusing to match energy, responding to what the situation needs rather than what the provocation invites. That's where dignity lives.

Why This Still Matters

Provocation invites matching tone or intensity. This feels justified in the moment. They started it. They set the terms. Why should you be the one to stay measured? Yet matching tone quickly erodes composure. Dignity weakens when reaction's shaped by what it opposes rather than what you've decided it should be.

How to Apply This Today

Notice situations where matching tone feels tempting. Someone criticizes you sharply, and the immediate impulse is to criticize back with equal force. Someone's dismissive, and you want to dismiss them right back. That impulse is natural. Following it usually makes things worse. Choosing a different register—measured where they're heated, calm where they're agitated—often preserves standing without conceding substance. You address the issue without becoming part of the problem.

"Escalation limits choice, restraint protects it."

Contentio optionem tollit, moderatio servat.

What Seneca Meant

Two trajectories. Escalation commits response fully and immediately, reducing room for adjustment. Restraint delays commitment just long enough for judgment to guide action. Choice survives where reaction pauses.

Why This Still Matters

Many outcomes feel inevitable only after escalation's occurred. Before that point, alternatives often exist—you just can't see them through the adrenaline and urgency. Restraint keeps those alternatives visible. It doesn't guarantee better outcomes, but it keeps them possible. Escalation forecloses them before you've explored whether they might work.

How to Apply This Today

Ask whether restraint's being used to protect choice or just to avoid confrontation. There's a difference. Restraint that protects choice is strategic—it keeps options open deliberately, maintaining flexibility until clarity emerges. That's valuable. Restraint that just delays inevitable confrontation without preserving meaningful alternatives isn't helpful. Protect choice. Don't just postpone conflict.

"The strongest response is the one that keeps judgment in command."

Imperium servatur cum iudicium praeest.

What Seneca Meant

Command forms the center of this observation. Response functions as an extension of judgment, not as reaction to provocation. When judgment leads, response remains deliberate and proportionate. Authority's preserved because action reflects choice, not pressure. The strength of a response lies in its alignment with reason, not in its intensity or speed or force.

Responses driven by impulse often feel powerful in the moment. They carry emotional weight. They feel decisive, immediate, strong. Yet they reduce credibility and limit future options because they demonstrate loss of command rather than possession of it. Real strength shows itself through measured response that reflects judgment choosing how to act, not emotion determining what must be said.

Why This Still Matters

When judgment remains in command, response carries weight without escalation. This steadiness tends to endure beyond the moment itself. People remember how you handled pressure, whether you maintained proportion, whether your actions reflected thought or just reaction. Authority that comes from composure lasts. Authority that comes from force evaporates the moment the force is removed.

How to Apply This Today

Before any significant response, ask: "Is judgment leading this, or is emotion driving it?" Not to eliminate emotion—that's impossible and unnecessary. But to check whether judgment's still in command, still able to guide what happens next. If emotion's driving, wait. Not because emotion's wrong, but because response shaped by it tends to create problems that outlast whatever satisfaction it provided in the moment. Strength comes from command, and command requires judgment to lead.

PART IV

AMBITION,
WEALTH,
AND STATUS

Chapter 7

Wanting More Without Losing Yourself

Ambition rarely announces itself as a problem. It shows up as effort, growth, or a serious approach to responsibility. Seneca treats it in these everyday terms. The concern begins when progress turns into self-definition, and personal worth starts to depend on outcomes that remain unstable.

Here, Seneca examines how desire can shift from direction to identity. Status, recognition, and visible success can slowly become reference points for value. The cost appears gradually: tension that settles in, habitual comparison, and a lingering sense that what exists is never sufficient. This shift happens through ordinary choices, repeated without pause or review.

The reflections that follow focus on a distinction: ambition can support a life, or a life can gradually reorganize itself around ambition. That difference affects how steady someone remains when results change or expectations fall apart.

The quotes in this chapter explore how to pursue aims while keeping judgment intact, preserving self-respect, and maintaining inner balance. The focus stays on ownership—knowing what belongs to you to guide, and what remains outside your control.

"You can make progress without turning success into your identity."

Non est vivere sed valere vita est.

What Seneca Meant

There's a boundary between effort and self-definition, and crossing it changes everything. Working toward goals, improving your position, using ability well—none of this requires making achievement the standard by which you measure your worth. But that's exactly what happens when progress stops being an activity and starts becoming a verdict on who you are.

The shift's subtle. At first, success is something you pursue. Over time, without noticing, it becomes something you need in order to feel intact. Your inner balance starts depending on results that remain unstable by nature. A good outcome lifts you. A bad one sinks you. Your sense of self rides the volatility instead of staying grounded.

Why This Still Matters

Modern life ties identity to visible outcomes constantly—titles, metrics, income, recognition. When those markers fluctuate, so does your sense of stability. The pressure doesn't come only from ambition itself, but from relying on external confirmation to feel settled. This creates a condition where effort never quite ends, because the reassurance it promises doesn't last.

You hit one milestone, feel relief for a day or a week, then immediately start working toward the next one because the calm you got from the first already wore off. The problem isn't the goals. It's that they're carrying weight they were never meant to carry—the weight of your entire sense of self-worth.

How to Apply This Today

Notice the difference between working toward something and using it as proof of personal value. When achievement's just an activity, failure doesn't threaten who you are—it's just feedback on an attempt. When achievement's become your identity, failure feels existential. That difference shows whether you're pursuing success or depending on it to feel whole.

"Desire becomes costly when it decides who you think you are."

Cupiditas animi imperium capit.

What Seneca Meant

Wanting more—status, comfort, influence—doesn't begin as excess. The shift occurs when desire starts to organize self-image and judgment. This happens gradually, without announcement. You begin evaluating days, choices, even relationships according to whether they advance a desired outcome. Desire moves from being a preference to being a lens through which everything gets seen.

Why This Still Matters

Constant comparison operates everywhere today. Social signals, professional benchmarks, curated success stories make desire feel urgent and continuous. When desire sets the terms of evaluation, satisfaction becomes temporary and attention narrows. The result is a steady undercurrent of restlessness, even when circumstances appear favorable.

You're always measuring, always checking where you stand relative to someone else, always feeling slightly behind or slightly anxious about losing whatever position you've gained. Desire's no longer directing your choices—it's governing your entire judgment system, deciding what counts as good and what doesn't.

How to Apply This Today

Ask whether desire informs your choices or governs your judgment. The first is healthy—you want something, so you work toward it. The second is corrosive—desire determines how you evaluate everything, including yourself. Seeing that difference clarifies why certain pursuits feel energizing while others quietly drain attention and calm.

"Ambition should serve your life, not reorganize it."

Ambitio inquietum facit.

What Seneca Meant

Proportion matters more than intensity. The question isn't how much you want, but how much space that wanting occupies. Ambition can support a coherent life when it stays in relation to other priorities. Trouble appears when it begins to reorder time, values, and self-respect around itself.

Why This Still Matters

Work and achievement often expand to fill available attention. Without deliberate awareness, ambition crowds out rest, reflection, and perspective. This doesn't require dramatic overwork—it happens through small adjustments that slowly tilt life toward constant evaluation and forward pressure.

Every conversation becomes about work. Every weekend gets spent thinking about Monday. Every moment of rest feels vaguely guilty, like time stolen from something more important. The person may still appear successful, yet feel increasingly constrained. Ambition's expanded beyond its proper role, from servant to master.

How to Apply This Today

Check whether ambition leaves room for steadiness. When a goal dictates every conversation, schedule, or measure of a "good" day, it's probably shaping life rather than supporting it. Ambition that serves you bends to accommodate other priorities. Ambition that's reorganized your life doesn't bend—everything else does.

"What you chase begins to control you once you depend on it for calm."

Quod cupimus, id nos tenet.

What Seneca Meant

Pursuits remain manageable as long as emotional balance doesn't rely on their outcome. The moment calm depends on getting something, that object gains leverage over judgment. Even reasonable goals start generating tension, because your state of mind's become conditional. Control gets handed over in return for the hope of reassurance.

This exchange happens quietly. You don't announce "I'm going to make my emotional stability dependent on this outcome." It just happens through repetition—every time you tell yourself you'll finally relax once this thing happens, you're training yourself to feel unsettled until it does.

Why This Still Matters

Many modern pressures promise relief once a milestone's reached—a promotion, financial buffer, public recognition. When calm's postponed to a future result, the present becomes a holding pattern. This creates ongoing unease, since the next condition's always uncertain or temporary.

How to Apply This Today

Notice what you believe will finally allow you to relax. That postponed calm—"I'll feel settled once I get this"—reveals where calm's been deferred to an outcome. Seeing that deferral loosens its grip on daily judgment. You can still pursue the goal. You just stop making your ability to feel okay dependent on achieving it.

"External gains don't settle an unsettled mind."

Non res sed animus inquietus est.

What Seneca Meant

Accumulation doesn't resolve inner strain. Discomfort often survives improved circumstances. Gains may change conditions, but they don't correct habits of judgment or attention.

Why This Still Matters

Modern culture reinforces the idea that better circumstances will bring relief. Yet many people experience rising pressure alongside rising success. The problem's subtle: when inner tension's treated as a resource issue, effort multiplies while clarity remains unchanged.

You get the promotion, the income increase, the recognition—and discover that the restlessness you thought would disappear just adapted to the new level. Now you're anxious about maintaining what you've gained, or about the next level up, or about whether you deserve what you have. The external changed. The internal patterns didn't.

When dissatisfaction comes from comparison, fear of loss, or constant evaluation, accumulation only increases what must be defended. More success means more to protect, more to worry about losing, more ways to feel inadequate despite objective achievement.

How to Apply This Today

Treat restlessness as a signal about judgment rather than circumstances. The question isn't "What do I need to get?" It's "What's driving this feeling of insufficiency?" Addressing that second question shifts where attention's placed, without requiring changes to external goals.

"Measure progress by stability, not by applause."

Recte factum ipsa rectitudine laudatur.

What Seneca Meant

Public response is a poor standard for private coherence. Applause depends on timing, audience, and visibility—all of which lie outside personal control. Stability, by contrast, reflects alignment between effort, values, and limits. The question isn't whether movement's noticed, but whether the person remains intact as they move forward.

Why This Still Matters

Many environments reward visibility more than consistency. Feedback loops based on recognition pull attention outward and fragment priorities. Over time, this makes judgment reactive and self-assessment unreliable. You start optimizing for what gets noticed rather than what actually matters to you.

How to Apply This Today

Compare how you feel after quiet progress versus public validation. Completing meaningful work that goes largely unseen often leaves more steadiness than praise that fades quickly. That difference reveals whether you're measuring progress by internal alignment or external approval.

"You lose balance when your sense of worth rises and falls with outcomes."

Eventus animos variant.

What Seneca Meant

Judgment becomes unstable when personal value's tied to results. Outcomes change for many reasons beyond effort, and when they serve as a measure of worth, your inner state follows their movement. Confidence grows fragile, because it depends on conditions that shift without warning.

This creates a pattern where self-assessment lacks an anchor. You're not grounded in anything stable—you're moving up or down with circumstances, feeling competent when things go well and worthless when they don't, regardless of whether your actual capabilities changed.

Why This Still Matters

Work, reputation, and financial results often come in cycles. When self-worth tracks these changes, emotional steadiness becomes difficult to maintain. Even favorable periods carry tension, since their end's anticipated. This produces a background unease that has little to do with present conditions.

How to Apply This Today

Notice where your sense of value seems most reactive. Which outcomes carry emotional weight beyond their practical importance? Seeing what's been allowed to act as a reference point for self-worth helps separate evaluation from identity. Results can matter without defining you.

"A full life isn't the same as a crowded one."

Plena vita est ordinata vita.

What Seneca Meant

Accumulation without proportion creates crowding, not fullness. A life can be busy, productive, and outwardly successful while still lacking coherence. When pursuits multiply without clear priority, effort spreads thin and satisfaction diminishes. What matters is order—choosing what deserves space rather than allowing everything to compete equally.

Why This Still Matters

Modern schedules often fill by default. Opportunities, requests, and ambitions stack up, each appearing reasonable on its own. Over time, the accumulation produces pressure rather than richness, as attention's divided and recovery becomes rare. You're doing lots of things, none of them particularly well, all of them draining you.

How to Apply This Today

Ask whether activity adds clarity or merely occupies time. Treating fullness as alignment rather than volume changes how choices are weighed. A full life has space to breathe. A crowded one doesn't, even when everything in it seems important.

"Ambition without limits trades freedom for motion."

Immodica cupido servitium parit.

What Seneca Meant

Movement without direction keeps you constantly advancing while gradually narrowing your options. Limits protect freedom by defining when effort stops and judgment resumes. Without them, momentum replaces choice. You stay active but increasingly constrained, driven more by continuation than intention.

Why This Still Matters

Many people remain in motion long after a goal's lost clarity. Progress continues because stopping feels risky or unclear. This creates fatigue without resolution, as movement itself becomes the justification. You can't remember why you started, but you can't bring yourself to stop either.

How to Apply This Today

Check whether momentum feels chosen or assumed. Continuing a demanding role simply because it's always led to the next step may signal motion replacing freedom. Real ambition knows when to stop. Motion disguised as ambition doesn't.

"The higher the stake you attach to success, the less steady you become."

Magna servitus est magna fortuna.

What Seneca Meant

Success becomes destabilizing when too much importance's assigned to it. As stakes rise, judgment narrows and tolerance for uncertainty decreases. Decisions begin carrying emotional consequences beyond their actual scope. Disproportionate importance quietly erodes steadiness, even when circumstances appear favorable.

You've made one outcome so important that everything else gets distorted around it. Small setbacks feel catastrophic. Ordinary challenges become threats. The pressure you've created by attaching massive significance to winning makes it nearly impossible to maintain perspective.

Why This Still Matters

Modern environments often reward escalation—bigger goals, larger risks, greater visibility. As the perceived stakes increase, so does pressure. This makes ordinary setbacks feel outsized and reduces the ability to respond calmly when plans shift.

How to Apply This Today

Notice where success has been given excessive weight. Which outcomes feel loaded with disproportionate significance? Seeing what's carrying too much can help restore measure without changing direction or effort. The goal can still matter. It just doesn't have to decide whether you're okay.

"You remain free when your life doesn't depend on winning."

Liber est cui nihil necesse est.

What Seneca Meant

Freedom comes from independence of judgment. Winning, achieving, or prevailing may be desirable, but they don't define whether a life holds together. When identity stays separate from outcomes, effort becomes cleaner and less anxious. This is freedom rooted in internal alignment rather than external confirmation.

You can pursue goals intensely without needing them to validate your existence. You can work hard, care about results, and still maintain composure when things don't go as planned. That's the freedom being described—not freedom from ambition, but freedom from depending on ambition's success to feel whole.

Why This Still Matters

Many pressures today frame life as a series of contests—career steps, social standing, performance metrics. When everything feels like a test, composure becomes difficult to maintain. Separating personal coherence from constant evaluation reduces this strain.

How to Apply This Today

Treat outcomes as events rather than verdicts. That distinction clarifies where freedom actually resides. Events happen—you win or lose, succeed or fail. Verdicts determine your worth. Events you can handle. Verdicts you carry. Seeing the difference often brings a quieter, more durable sense of balance.

Chapter 8

Using What You Have Well

Possessions tend to feel neutral at first, simply part of the background of daily life, until they begin to shape decisions, expectations, and reactions in ways that are easy to overlook. Seneca approaches wealth from this angle. He's less interested in how much a person owns than in how ownership influences judgment, calm, and readiness for change.

In this chapter, attention turns to use rather than accumulation. What matters is the relationship a person has with what they possess, especially when circumstances shift. Wealth can support independence, or it can quietly increase anxiety by creating more to protect, maintain, and justify.

Seneca treats material resources as a test of character rather than a measure of success. How easily someone can enjoy what they have without clinging to it reveals more than the size of their holdings. The reflections that follow focus on steadiness—whether a person remains composed when conditions improve, and equally steady when they don't.

These quotes consider ownership as a responsibility of judgment. The aim is to clarify how resources can be held lightly enough to be useful, without allowing them to define security, identity, or peace of mind.

"What you own should support your life, not weigh on it."

Res possessae ad usum, non ad onus sunt.

What Seneca Meant

The relationship between possession and judgment determines whether ownership feels light or heavy. When possessions begin demanding constant attention, protection, or justification, they stop serving their original purpose. The problem doesn't lie in having resources—it lies in allowing them to occupy more mental space than they deserve.

This shift happens gradually. You acquire something useful. Over time, maintaining it becomes a concern. Then protecting it. Then justifying it to yourself or others. Before long, what was supposed to make life easier has become another source of background stress. The possession hasn't changed. Your relationship with it has.

Why This Still Matters

Modern life encourages accumulation without reflection. Subscriptions, assets, obligations, and upgrades add up gradually, each one manageable on its own. Over time, they can crowd attention and create a background sense of maintenance stress, even when nothing's actively wrong.

You're not drowning in possessions—you're just carrying a low-grade burden from managing, tracking, protecting, and maintaining everything you've accumulated. The weight comes not from any single thing, but from the collective demand on your attention.

How to Apply This Today

Notice which possessions feel supportive and which feel demanding. That difference clarifies whether resources are lightening life or quietly loading it. Supportive things serve their purpose without requiring constant thought. Demanding things occupy mental space beyond their actual utility. Seeing the difference often reveals where simplification would help.

"Wealth tests your judgment more than your circumstances."

Divitiae mores detegunt.

What Seneca Meant

Abundance reveals habits of mind. Increased means don't automatically improve judgment—they often expose existing tendencies. Comfort can amplify fear of loss, attachment, or comparison just as easily as it can support ease and generosity. Wealth, in this sense, functions as a mirror rather than a solution. It shows how a person relates to control, security, and sufficiency.

Why This Still Matters

Greater access to options often increases decision pressure. With more to choose from, manage, or preserve, attention fragments more easily. The expectation that improved circumstances will simplify life frequently gives way to new forms of concern and vigilance. More wealth often means more complexity, not less.

How to Apply This Today

Ask whether resources feel stabilizing or mentally consuming. Observing how judgment shifts as circumstances improve can reveal what actually governs peace of mind. If better circumstances create new anxieties at the same rate they solve old problems, the issue isn't resources—it's how you relate to having them.

"Possessions are easiest to use when you're ready to lose them."

Facile habet qui facile amittit.

What Seneca Meant

Ease comes from flexibility of mind. When you can imagine loss without inner collapse, possessions remain tools instead of anchors. Readiness to let go doesn't imply indifference—it reflects clarity about what does and doesn't define you. This stance keeps judgment free even in favorable conditions.

Why This Still Matters

Many people enjoy what they have while simultaneously worrying about its disappearance. This tension dulls satisfaction and sharpens anxiety. The enjoyment becomes conditional, shadowed by protection and anticipation of loss. You can't fully appreciate what you're constantly afraid of losing.

How to Apply This Today

Notice how much mental effort goes into safeguarding what you own. When maintaining a certain lifestyle requires constant vigilance, it may be shaping attention more than supporting it. The tighter the grip, the heavier the burden. Holding things lightly doesn't mean caring less—it means not letting possessions determine your state of mind.

"What you keep should remain easy to put down."

Facile est deponere quod recte tenetur.

What Seneca Meant

Healthy ownership doesn't tighten the grip of the mind. When something's held with excessive care, fear enters the picture and judgment narrows. Ease, by contrast, signals proportion. You can enjoy what's present without constant guarding or rehearsal of loss. Internal looseness keeps ownership from becoming a source of strain.

Why This Still Matters

Many modern pressures come from maintenance rather than lack. Managing assets, commitments, and standards can quietly consume attention. When holding something requires vigilance, calm becomes conditional. The pressure doesn't come from what's owned, but from how tightly it's mentally secured.

How to Apply This Today

Notice which things feel simple to carry and which feel fragile. That contrast often reveals where attachment's grown heavier than usefulness. Easy things can be set down without drama when circumstances change. Heavy things can't—they demand constant protection, creating stress that outlasts any benefit they provide.

"You're richer when you need less to feel secure."

In summa copia est animus modicus.

What Seneca Meant

Security depends less on quantity than on expectations. When needs expand alongside resources, satisfaction remains out of reach. A moderated sense of what's enough allows resources to do their job without creating new demands.

Why This Still Matters

Rising standards often move faster than rising means. As expectations adjust upward, security feels postponed. This creates a cycle where improvement fails to deliver relief, and attention stays fixed on what remains missing. You get more, need more, feel no more secure than you did before.

How to Apply This Today

Ask whether security feels settled or deferred. Seeing where expectations have quietly expanded clarifies why comfort sometimes feels incomplete despite objective improvement. The question isn't "What more do I need?" It's "Why doesn't what I have feel like enough?" Addressing that second question often provides more relief than acquiring more.

"What you own should answer to you, not the other way around."

Dominari res, non servire.

What Seneca Meant

Ownership reverses when possessions begin dictating choices, schedules, or emotional reactions. Resources are meant to support agency. When they start setting terms, the person adapts around them. This shift often happens gradually, through accommodation rather than decision. Control changes hands without being noticed.

You buy something to make life easier. Then you have to maintain it. Then organize around it. Then adjust your schedule to accommodate it. Then justify keeping it. Before long, you're serving the possession more than it's serving you.

Why This Still Matters

Modern life offers many conveniences that also impose upkeep. Tools, properties, and commitments can quietly restructure time and attention. Over time, this reduces flexibility and increases background pressure. What started as optional becomes obligatory without you choosing the shift.

How to Apply This Today

Notice what regularly forces adjustment. When maintaining possessions determines daily priorities, they may be shaping life more than serving it. The question isn't whether you can afford to keep something—it's whether keeping it costs more attention than it provides value.

"Use what you have without letting it set your mood."

Res ad usum, animus ad aequitatem.

What Seneca Meant

Possessions begin mattering too much when they start influencing calm, confidence, or irritation. Enjoyment becomes unstable when mood rises or falls with access, condition, or performance of what you own. Emotional balance gets outsourced to external things. When that happens, judgment follows circumstance instead of remaining settled.

Why This Still Matters

Modern life encourages emotional feedback from material conditions—comfort when things work smoothly, frustration when they don't. This creates small but frequent disturbances that accumulate. The issue's rarely the object itself, but the expectation that it should regulate how you feel.

How to Apply This Today

Notice which possessions seem to influence emotional tone. Seeing where mood depends on things working a certain way often restores a quieter sense of control. Things can serve you without determining whether you're okay. That separation's worth establishing, because otherwise every malfunction or imperfection becomes a personal disruption.

"Possessions serve best when they stay in their place."

Ordine suo res prosunt.

What Seneca Meant

Usefulness is a matter of placement—each thing having a defined role and limit. When possessions begin spilling into areas of identity, priority, or self-assessment, they lose proportion. Mental organization keeps resources as tools instead of reference points for value or security.

Why This Still Matters

Distraction often comes from blurred boundaries. When material concerns mix with self-worth or attention meant for relationships and judgment, pressure increases. Life feels cluttered even without visible excess. The problem's not too many things—it's things occupying space they shouldn't.

How to Apply This Today

Ask whether resources occupy their role or drift into areas where they don't belong. That awareness often brings order without requiring reduction. Your possessions can serve practical purposes without becoming markers of identity or security. Keeping them in their proper place—as tools, not as definitions of self—reduces the burden they carry.

"You own things more lightly when you expect change."

Omnia mutabilia sunt.

What Seneca Meant

Change is constant, not exceptional. When this is understood, possessions are enjoyed with flexibility rather than fear. Expecting change doesn't diminish appreciation—it keeps attachment from hardening. You can value what you have without needing it to last forever.

Why This Still Matters

Many pressures arise from treating current conditions as fixed. When change arrives—as it often does—it feels disruptive rather than ordinary. This amplifies stress around loss, replacement, or adjustment. The disruption comes less from the change itself than from the assumption it shouldn't happen.

How to Apply This Today

Notice reactions when something owned needs replacing or no longer fits. Irritation that lingers longer than the inconvenience itself may signal an expectation of permanence that was never realistic. Everything changes eventually. Expecting that doesn't make you care less—it just makes the inevitable transitions easier to handle.

"Enjoy what you have without letting it promise permanence."

Nulla res diu tenetur.

What Seneca Meant

Enjoyment's cleanest when it's not tied to assumptions about duration. Possessions can be used fully while remaining understood as temporary. When permanence is expected, enjoyment quietly tightens into vigilance. The mental posture that allows appreciation without the added burden of guarding against change creates more actual satisfaction than any amount of protection ever could.

Why This Still Matters

Many modern pressures come from treating present conditions as guarantees. Comfort, access, and convenience are often assumed to continue. When they shift, the disruption feels larger than it needs to be. Expectation, more than loss itself, amplifies the impact.

How to Apply This Today

Notice where enjoyment carries an unspoken promise about the future. Seeing that expectation can soften reactions when conditions inevitably adjust. You can appreciate what you have today without requiring it to last forever. That separation—between enjoying and expecting to keep—creates a steadier form of satisfaction.

"You use wealth well when it leaves you unchanged."

Recte utitur qui aequus manet.

What Seneca Meant

Steadiness is the measure of good use. Resources are handled well when they don't distort character, judgment, or emotional balance. Increased means test whether a person remains consistent across circumstances. The aim is coherence—being the same person with more, just as with less.

This doesn't mean wealth shouldn't improve your life. It means improvement shouldn't require becoming someone else. The person who handles abundance well maintains the same priorities, values, and emotional balance they had before. The circumstances changed. They didn't.

Why This Still Matters

Shifts in income or comfort often bring subtle changes in behavior and priorities. Without awareness, these shifts can pull attention outward and alter standards quietly. Steadiness becomes harder to maintain as options multiply. You start optimizing for different things, caring about different markers, comparing yourself to different people—and the person you were fades without you choosing the transformation.

How to Apply This Today

Ask whether changes in circumstance alter how you relate to time, people, or yourself. Treating consistency as the reference point keeps resources in their proper role. Wealth should serve the life you're building, not rebuild you around itself.

PART VI

LIVING WELL, CONSISTENTLY

Chapter 9

Integrity When No One Is Watching

Character becomes most visible in moments that leave no trace—choices made without witnesses, decisions that never require explanation, standards applied only because someone chooses to keep them. Seneca pays close attention to this quiet territory, where conduct is shaped by internal agreement rather than external response.

In this chapter, the focus shifts to consistency across situations. Public behavior is often guided by expectation and consequence. Private behavior reveals what actually governs judgment when incentives fall away. Seneca treats this contrast as practical rather than moral. It shows where a person's sense of order truly resides.

The reflections that follow examine how small, unobserved decisions accumulate into a stable or unstable self. Integrity, as Seneca understands it, is not a performance. It is the ability to remain aligned when there is nothing to gain and nothing to prove.

These quotes explore how steadiness is maintained in the absence of recognition, pressure, or reward. What emerges is a view of character shaped less by circumstances than by the standards a person continues to apply in silence.

"Your character shows most clearly when no response is expected."

Qualis quisque est, cum nemo videt.

What Seneca Meant

The focus here is on conditions without witnesses. Seneca observes that judgment becomes most honest when external response disappears. Without praise, consequence, or comparison, choices reflect what a person actually values. This is where habits operate without adjustment or display. Seneca is pointing to a quiet test: when nothing follows a decision, what standard still applies?

Why This Still Matters

Much of modern behavior is shaped by feedback—messages, metrics, visibility. When response becomes the reference point, attention shifts outward and standards adjust accordingly. Moments without feedback can feel empty or unclear, yet they reveal where judgment truly rests.

How to Apply This Today

It is worth noticing how decisions feel when they carry no audience. Seeing which standards remain active in private can clarify what has real authority in daily life.

"Consistency matters more than reputation."

Constans animus, non fama.

What Seneca Meant

Attention is drawn to alignment across settings. Seneca distinguishes between how one is seen and how one remains. Reputation depends on context and circulation; consistency depends on internal agreement. When standards vary with audience, judgment fragments. Seneca is concerned with coherence—being the same person across situations, whether observed or unseen.

Why This Still Matters

Public signals often reward performance over steadiness. This can encourage subtle shifts in behavior depending on who is present. Over time, maintaining multiple versions of oneself adds strain and weakens trust in one's own judgment.

How to Apply This Today

A useful distinction is whether behavior changes with visibility. Treating consistency as the reference point can reduce the effort spent managing perception.

"Private choices shape the person you become."

Ex minimis moribus animus fingitur.

What Seneca Meant

What is examined here is accumulation. Seneca notes that character forms through repeated, ordinary decisions rather than dramatic moments. Small choices made without notice settle into habit. These habits, taken together, shape how judgment operates under pressure. Seneca is highlighting how the unseen gradually becomes decisive.

Why This Still Matters

Daily life is filled with minor decisions that seem inconsequential. When attention is scattered, these moments pass without reflection. Over time, the pattern they form influences how a person responds when stakes rise.

How to Apply This Today

One way to see this is to notice how you handle minor commitments that no one tracks—for example, whether you follow through on tasks only you will notice. Those moments often reveal the standards that quietly guide larger decisions.

"What you approve in private is what you truly stand for."

Probatio conscientiae.

What Seneca Meant

The focus here is approval rather than appearance. Seneca points to the quiet act of agreeing with oneself. When no justification is required, choices reveal what a person actually endorses. Approval given in private carries more weight than any public statement, because it reflects judgment without adjustment. Seneca is observing where standards are set and maintained—inside the mind, before any audience enters the picture.

Why This Still Matters

Modern life offers many ways to explain, frame, or soften decisions once they are visible. This can blur the line between conviction and convenience. Private approval strips those layers away and shows what a person is willing to live with internally, even when nothing needs to be defended.

How to Apply This Today

It is worth noticing which actions feel settled afterward and which require mental explanation. That contrast often reveals where genuine agreement exists.

"Integrity holds when convenience loses its appeal."

Integritas in opportunitate probatur.

What Seneca Meant

Attention is drawn to moments of ease. Seneca observes that integrity is tested when taking a shortcut would carry no immediate cost. Convenience invites small departures from standards that seem harmless in isolation. Over time, these adjustments reshape judgment. Seneca is not focused on single decisions, but on how repeated ease alters what feels acceptable.

Why This Still Matters

Time pressure and overload make convenience attractive. Small compromises often appear reasonable when schedules are tight and accountability is low. Yet these moments quietly influence how standards are applied later, especially under greater pressure.

How to Apply This Today

A useful distinction is whether convenience changes what feels permissible. Seeing where ease begins to guide judgment can clarify which standards are genuinely held.

"You reveal your character when no one benefits from your restraint."

Virtus sine teste.

What Seneca Meant

What is examined here is restraint without reward. Seneca notes that many forms of self-control are reinforced by recognition or consequence. When neither is present, restraint becomes purely internal. This is where character operates without support. Seneca is highlighting a form of discipline that exists only because a person chooses it.

Why This Still Matters

Many settings reward visible compliance more than quiet consistency. When restraint brings no advantage, it can feel unnecessary. Over time, this erodes the habit of acting according to internal standards rather than external incentives.

How to Apply This Today

One way to see this is to notice how you handle minor choices that offer an easy gain without downside—for example, cutting corners on work that will never be reviewed. These moments often show where restraint truly comes from.

"What you excuse in yourself becomes part of you."

Excusatio vitium alit.

What Seneca Meant

The focus here is tolerance turned inward. Seneca observes that repeated self-excusing shapes character over time. When judgment bends to accommodate small lapses, those adjustments settle into habit. What begins as an exception gradually becomes familiar. Seneca is not concerned with isolated mistakes, but with what a person quietly permits to stand without review.

Why This Still Matters

Modern pressure often encourages self-leniency framed as necessity. Fatigue, urgency, and overload make justification easy to supply. Over time, this can blur personal standards, especially when no external correction is present.

How to Apply This Today

It is worth noticing which behaviors are routinely explained away. Seeing where explanation replaces evaluation can clarify how standards are being maintained—or softened.

"A steady mind does not depend on being observed."

Animus sibi sufficit.

What Seneca Meant

Attention is drawn to internal sufficiency. Seneca points to a form of steadiness that holds without reinforcement. When judgment relies on being seen or affirmed, it weakens in private. A self-sufficient mind maintains orientation regardless of visibility. Seneca is describing independence of judgment rather than withdrawal from others.

Why This Still Matters

Visibility has become a frequent source of validation. Feedback loops encourage alignment with response rather than principle. When observation fades, direction can fade with it, leaving uncertainty about what actually matters.

How to Apply This Today

A useful distinction is whether clarity remains when attention from others drops away. Treating internal agreement as sufficient can reduce reliance on constant confirmation.

"Small compromises quietly reset your standards."

Minuta vitia crescunt.

What Seneca Meant

What is examined here is gradual adjustment. Seneca notes that standards rarely collapse at once. They shift through minor allowances that feel insignificant in isolation. Each compromise recalibrates what feels acceptable. Over time, the original standard becomes distant, replaced by a more convenient one.

Why This Still Matters

Daily life is full of minor decisions made quickly and without review. Under time pressure, these moments seem harmless. Yet their accumulation shapes how judgment operates when larger choices appear.

How to Apply This Today

One way to see this is to notice how often you allow small exceptions for the sake of ease—for example, skipping careful work on tasks that no one else will see. Those moments often indicate where standards are being quietly reset.

"Integrity is what remains when excuses run out."

Integritas manet.

What Seneca Meant

The focus here is endurance of judgment. Seneca is concerned with what holds once justification loses force. When reasons fall away—fatigue, pressure, circumstance—what remains shows the real standard at work. Integrity, in this sense, is not sustained by argument. It persists because it has been settled internally. Seneca is describing a steadiness that does not require continual reinforcement to stay intact.

Why This Still Matters

Modern life offers many explanations for compromise. When those explanations are exhausted, people often discover whether their standards were conditional or durable. This moment of exposure is quiet, yet revealing. It shows whether judgment has been anchored or merely supported by circumstance.

How to Apply This Today

A useful distinction is whether standards feel dependent on favorable conditions. Treating integrity as what remains after justification fades can clarify where judgment truly rests.

"You keep your character by keeping your agreements with yourself."

Pacta animi servantur.

What Seneca Meant

Attention is drawn to internal commitment. Seneca views character as the result of promises kept privately, long before they are tested publicly. Agreements made with oneself—about effort, fairness, restraint—shape conduct even when no reminder appears. When these agreements are honored consistently, judgment stays coherent. Seneca is highlighting self-trust as a foundation of integrity.

Why This Still Matters

Many pressures today pull attention outward, toward response and approval. This can weaken private commitments that lack visibility. When internal agreements erode, consistency becomes harder to maintain across changing situations.

How to Apply This Today

It is worth noticing which personal commitments remain active without reinforcement. Seeing where self-agreement still guides behavior can bring a quiet sense of reliability and calm.

Chapter 10

Facing Difficulty Without Complaining

Character becomes most visible in moments that leave no trace—choices made without witnesses, decisions that never require explanation, standards applied only because someone chooses to keep them. Seneca pays close attention to this quiet territory, where conduct's shaped by internal agreement rather than external response.

In this chapter, the focus shifts to consistency across situations. Public behavior's often guided by expectation and consequence. Private behavior reveals what actually governs judgment when incentives fall away. Seneca treats this contrast as practical rather than moral. It shows where a person's sense of order truly resides.

The reflections that follow examine how small, unobserved decisions accumulate into a stable or unstable self. Integrity, as Seneca understands it, isn't a performance. It's the ability to remain aligned when there's nothing to gain and nothing to prove.

These quotes explore how steadiness is maintained in the absence of recognition, pressure, or reward. What emerges is a view of character shaped less by circumstances than by the standards a person continues to apply in silence.

"Your character shows most clearly when no response is expected."

Qualis quisque est, cum nemo videt.

What Seneca Meant

Judgment becomes most honest when external response disappears. Without praise, consequence, or comparison, choices reflect what you actually value. This is where habits operate without adjustment or display. When nothing follows a decision—no feedback, no recognition, no consequence—what standard still applies? That question reveals character more clearly than any public action ever could.

Why This Still Matters

Much of modern behavior's shaped by feedback—messages, metrics, visibility. When response becomes the reference point, attention shifts outward and standards adjust accordingly. You start optimizing for what gets noticed rather than what matters. Moments without feedback can feel empty or unclear, yet they reveal where judgment truly rests.

How to Apply This Today

Notice how decisions feel when they carry no audience. Which standards remain active in private? Seeing what holds when no one's watching clarifies what has real authority in your daily life, versus what's maintained primarily for show.

"Consistency matters more than reputation."

Constans animus, non fama.

What Seneca Meant

There's a distinction between how you're seen and how you remain. Reputation depends on context and circulation—it shifts with audience and circumstance. Consistency depends on internal agreement. When standards vary with audience, judgment fragments. You become different people in different contexts, and eventually lose track of which version is actually you.

Why This Still Matters

Public signals often reward performance over steadiness. This encourages subtle shifts in behavior depending on who's present. Over time, maintaining multiple versions of yourself adds strain and weakens trust in your own judgment. You're constantly code-switching, adjusting, managing perceptions—and the cognitive load quietly accumulates.

How to Apply This Today

Ask whether your behavior changes with visibility. If you'd handle a situation differently when someone's watching versus when they're not, that gap reveals where consistency needs attention. Treating consistency as the reference point reduces the effort spent managing perception.

"Private choices shape the person you become."

Ex minimis moribus animus fingitur.

What Seneca Meant

Character forms through repeated, ordinary decisions rather than dramatic moments. Small choices made without notice settle into habit. These habits, taken together, shape how judgment operates under pressure. The unseen gradually becomes decisive. You're not built by your biggest decisions—you're built by the thousand small ones no one sees.

Why This Still Matters

Daily life's filled with minor decisions that seem inconsequential. When attention's scattered, these moments pass without reflection. Over time, the pattern they form influences how you respond when stakes rise. The habits you build in private are the ones that show up publicly when pressure hits.

How to Apply This Today

Notice how you handle minor commitments that no one tracks. Do you follow through on tasks only you will notice? Those moments often reveal the standards that quietly guide larger decisions. If you cut corners when no one's looking, you're training judgment to prioritize convenience over principle.

"What you approve in private is what you truly stand for."

Probatio conscientiae.

What Seneca Meant

There's the quiet act of agreeing with yourself. When no justification's required, choices reveal what you actually endorse. Approval given in private carries more weight than any public statement, because it reflects judgment without adjustment. This is where standards are set and maintained—inside the mind, before any audience enters the picture.

Why This Still Matters

Modern life offers many ways to explain, frame, or soften decisions once they're visible. This can blur the line between conviction and convenience. Private approval strips those layers away and shows what you're willing to live with internally, even when nothing needs to be defended.

How to Apply This Today

Notice which actions feel settled afterward and which require mental explanation. Actions that need no internal justification reflect genuine agreement. Actions that require you to explain them to yourself afterward reveal misalignment between your standards and your choices.

"Integrity holds when convenience loses its appeal."

Integritas in opportunitate probatur.

What Seneca Meant

Integrity's tested when taking a shortcut would carry no immediate cost. Convenience invites small departures from standards that seem harmless in isolation. Over time, these adjustments reshape judgment. The focus isn't on single decisions, but on how repeated ease alters what feels acceptable.

Why This Still Matters

Time pressure and overload make convenience attractive. Small compromises often appear reasonable when schedules are tight and accountability's low. Yet these moments quietly influence how standards are applied later, especially under greater pressure. Each convenient shortcut trains judgment to prioritize ease over principle.

How to Apply This Today

Ask whether convenience changes what feels permissible. If your standards shift based on how easy the alternative is, they're not actually standards—they're preferences that bend under pressure. Seeing where ease begins to guide judgment clarifies which standards are genuinely held versus which are negotiable.

"You reveal your character when no one benefits from your restraint."

Virtus sine teste.

What Seneca Meant

Many forms of self-control are reinforced by recognition or consequence. When neither's present, restraint becomes purely internal. This is where character operates without support—discipline that exists only because you choose it, not because anyone's watching or rewarding it.

Why This Still Matters

Many settings reward visible compliance more than quiet consistency. When restraint brings no advantage, it can feel unnecessary. Over time, this erodes the habit of acting according to internal standards rather than external incentives. You start asking "What's the point?" when the answer should be "Because this is who I am."

How to Apply This Today

Notice how you handle minor choices that offer an easy gain without downside. Cutting corners on work that'll never be reviewed, taking shortcuts no one will notice—these moments show where restraint truly comes from. If it only exists when someone's watching, it's not really yours.

"What you excuse in yourself becomes part of you."

Excusatio vitium alit.

What Seneca Meant

Repeated self-excusing shapes character over time. When judgment bends to accommodate small lapses, those adjustments settle into habit. What begins as an exception gradually becomes familiar. The concern isn't with isolated mistakes, but with what you quietly permit to stand without review.

Why This Still Matters

Modern pressure often encourages self-leniency framed as necessity. Fatigue, urgency, and overload make justification easy to supply. Over time, this can blur personal standards, especially when no external correction's present. Every excuse you accept becomes a small vote for the person you're becoming.

How to Apply This Today

Notice which behaviors are routinely explained away. "Just this once" becomes a pattern when repeated. Seeing where explanation replaces evaluation clarifies how standards are being maintained—or softened. The question isn't whether you made a mistake. It's whether you're holding yourself accountable for it.

"A steady mind doesn't depend on being observed."

Animus sibi sufficit.

What Seneca Meant

There's a form of steadiness that holds without reinforcement. When judgment relies on being seen or affirmed, it weakens in private. A self-sufficient mind maintains orientation regardless of visibility. This describes independence of judgment rather than withdrawal from others.

Why This Still Matters

Visibility's become a frequent source of validation. Feedback loops encourage alignment with response rather than principle. When observation fades, direction can fade with it, leaving uncertainty about what actually matters. You're steady when people are watching, adrift when they're not.

How to Apply This Today

Ask whether clarity remains when attention from others drops away. If your sense of direction depends on constant confirmation, steadiness becomes fragile. Treating internal agreement as sufficient reduces reliance on external validation while maintaining genuine connection with others.

"Small compromises quietly reset your standards."

Minuta vitia crescunt.

What Seneca Meant

Standards rarely collapse at once. They shift through minor allowances that feel insignificant in isolation. Each compromise recalibrates what feels acceptable. Over time, the original standard becomes distant, replaced by a more convenient one. You don't abandon your principles dramatically—you adjust them gradually until they're unrecognizable.

Why This Still Matters

Daily life's full of minor decisions made quickly and without review. Under time pressure, these moments seem harmless. Yet their accumulation shapes how judgment operates when larger choices appear. Small compromises today become the baseline for bigger ones tomorrow.

How to Apply This Today

Notice how often you allow small exceptions for the sake of ease. Skipping careful work on tasks no one else will see, taking shortcuts when time's tight—those moments often indicate where standards are being quietly reset. Each exception doesn't just violate the standard. It moves it.

"Integrity is what remains when excuses run out."

Integritas manet.

What Seneca Meant

What holds once justification loses force reveals the real standard at work. When reasons fall away—fatigue, pressure, circumstance—what remains shows what's actually guiding you. Integrity, in this sense, isn't sustained by argument. It persists because it's been settled internally, requiring no continual reinforcement to stay intact.

Why This Still Matters

Modern life offers many explanations for compromise. When those explanations are exhausted, you discover whether your standards were conditional or durable. This moment of exposure's quiet, yet revealing. It shows whether judgment's been anchored or merely supported by favorable circumstances.

How to Apply This Today

Ask whether your standards feel dependent on favorable conditions. Do they hold when you're tired, stressed, or rushed? If not, they're not really standards—they're aspirations that collapse under pressure. Treating integrity as what remains after justification fades clarifies where judgment truly rests.

"You keep your character by keeping your agreements with yourself."

Pacta animi servantur.

What Seneca Meant

Character results from promises kept privately, long before they're tested publicly. Agreements made with yourself—about effort, fairness, restraint—shape conduct even when no reminder appears. When these agreements are honored consistently, judgment stays coherent. Self-trust becomes the foundation of integrity.

Why This Still Matters

Many pressures today pull attention outward, toward response and approval. This can weaken private commitments that lack visibility. When internal agreements erode, consistency becomes harder to maintain across changing situations. You start breaking promises to yourself, and eventually stop trusting your own word.

How to Apply This Today

Notice which personal commitments remain active without reinforcement. Do you keep promises to yourself the way you'd keep them to others? Seeing where self-agreement still guides behavior can bring a quiet sense of reliability and calm. Your relationship with yourself sets the template for all your other relationships.

PART VI

LIVING WELL, CONSISTENTLY

Chapter 11

A Life That Holds Together

Daily reflection rarely looks significant in the moment—it tends to appear modest, easily postponed, and difficult to justify when time feels scarce. Yet Seneca treats it as one of the few practices that quietly protects clarity across changing conditions. He doesn't approach reflection as self-examination in the dramatic sense, nor as a search for insight or resolution. It functions instead as a form of upkeep—attention returned to itself before habits harden unchecked.

In this chapter, reflection's presented as a way of staying oriented rather than improving performance. Seneca understands that judgment drifts under pressure. Small reactions go unexamined, priorities blur, and standards soften without notice. Brief, regular review allows these shifts to be seen while they're still minor and easy to correct.

The reflections that follow focus on adjustment without self-reproach. Seneca's interested in noticing patterns, not assigning blame. Reflection, in this sense, preserves steadiness by keeping experience from accumulating unexamined weight.

These quotes explore how clarity's maintained over time through quiet attention. What emerges is a view of reflection as maintenance rather than transformation—an ordinary act that helps a life continue to hold together under ordinary strain.

"A short review keeps small errors from settling in."

Levis inspectio corrigit.

What Seneca Meant

Daily review functions as prevention through attention. Minor lapses, unexamined reactions, and quiet inconsistencies tend to accumulate when left alone. A brief look back brings them into view while they're still light—before they solidify into habits or blind spots. Correction works best when it remains close to the action that produced it.

Timing matters. The longer something goes unnoticed, the more normal it begins to feel.

Why This Still Matters

Modern days move quickly and leave little space for pause. Reactions pass into routine without being registered. Over time, this creates friction that feels sudden even though it developed gradually. Regular review interrupts that pattern by keeping experience from slipping by unnoticed. The errors aren't dramatic. They're small—but small things compound silently.

How to Apply This Today

Check for small misalignments while they're still minor. Five minutes at day's end—not an hour, just five—can keep judgment from carrying unresolved residue forward. The question isn't "Did I do everything right?" It's "What slipped today that I'd rather not repeat?"

"Reflection maintains direction when days blur together."

Animus revocandus est.

What Seneca Meant

Pressure compresses days into sequences of response. Without reflection, direction's assumed rather than confirmed. Brief review restores a sense of bearing by reconnecting actions with standards. This isn't analysis—it's a return to reference points that might otherwise fade during routine. Orientation depends on checking periodically whether you're still headed where you intended to go.

Why This Still Matters

Busy schedules often replace intention with momentum. When days resemble one another, priorities can drift without being noticed. You're moving, responding, completing tasks—but the direction those tasks point toward may have shifted without deliberate decision. Reflection reintroduces distinction, helping prevent gradual misalignment driven by pace alone.

You think you're on track because nothing's obviously wrong. Review reveals whether that assumption's accurate, or whether you've been maintaining motion while losing bearing.

How to Apply This Today

How does a day feel after it ends? Work completed efficiently yet leaving you feeling pulled in many directions signals misalignment. A short review clarifies whether effort followed priorities or simply kept pace—one builds toward something, the other just maintains motion.

"Correction works best before self-criticism arrives."

Emendatio sine acerbitate.

What Seneca Meant

There's a difference between review and reproach. When reflection becomes harsh, it discourages return. When it stays neutral, it invites honesty. Self-criticism can overshadow observation quickly, turning maintenance into avoidance. The aim of review's clarity, not judgment of character. Seeing what happened matters more than deciding whether you're adequate.

Why This Still Matters

Many people associate reflection with fault-finding. This makes it easy to postpone or abandon altogether. As a result, patterns continue unchecked until they feel heavier and harder to face. The weight comes not from the patterns themselves, but from delayed attention that allows them to compound unaddressed.

How to Apply This Today

Reflection that feels charged rather than approachable won't last. Keep review neutral—simple observation without judgment. When looking back feels like preparing for self-reproach, that tone eventually makes the practice something to avoid, defeating the purpose entirely.

"Review keeps judgment from drifting unnoticed."

Iudicium revocatur.

What Seneca Meant

Judgment rarely collapses suddenly. It shifts gradually, shaped by repetition and pressure. Without periodic review, these shifts go unseen and begin to feel normal. Reflection brings judgment back into view—not to correct everything, but to restore awareness of where it's moved. The concern's drift, not error. Small changes in what feels acceptable accumulate silently until they've altered standards without deliberate choice.

Why This Still Matters

Modern life encourages continuous response. Decisions are made quickly, often under mild but constant pressure. Over time, this pace can alter priorities without deliberate choice. Drift becomes visible only when it's already settled. Review catches movement while it's still minor—before recalibration requires significant effort.

How to Apply This Today

Ask whether recent decisions still align with what feels settled and deliberate. If standards have quietly shifted toward what's convenient or expected rather than chosen, seeing that drift early makes adjustment simple. Wait too long, and the gap between intention and practice becomes its own problem.

"Reflection keeps habit from standing in for choice."

Consuetudo subrepit.

What Seneca Meant

Habit brings ease and speed, but it also dulls awareness. When actions repeat without being reviewed, they begin operating on their own authority. Choice gives way to continuation. The pattern becomes self-justifying—you do it because you've always done it, and you've always done it, so it must be right. That interruption—however brief—allows judgment back into the picture. Not every habit needs changing, but every habit benefits from being seen occasionally, to verify it still reflects choice rather than just inertia.

Why This Still Matters

Busy routines often reward efficiency over awareness. As days fill, repeated actions feel justified simply because they're familiar. Over time, this can narrow flexibility and reduce the sense of authorship over one's own conduct. You're acting from pattern rather than decision, and the distinction fades without periodic check-ins.

How to Apply This Today

When actions continue mainly because they're established rather than chosen, habit's replaced decision-making. Seeing that replacement clarifies whether the pattern still serves you or whether it's just inertia wearing the appearance of intention.

"Looking back briefly keeps the day from hardening."

Dies resolvitur.

What Seneca Meant

Days leave residue—small tensions, reactions, and judgments that settle if left untouched. Reflection softens this residue before it sets. The aim isn't review for its own sake, but release. By looking back while the day's still close, experience remains flexible rather than fixed. Small moments that might otherwise harden into resentment or unresolved tension can be seen, acknowledged, and set down.

Why This Still Matters

Days often end with unresolved moments that carry forward unnoticed. Over time, these moments stack, creating a sense of weight that feels larger than any single event. Reflection limits that buildup. It's not about solving everything—it's about preventing accumulation.

How to Apply This Today

If the next morning feels lighter after an evening review, that's evidence the practice works. Small tensions didn't carry over. The review doesn't need elaboration—even a few minutes creates separation between experience and residue.

"Reflection keeps effort from turning rigid."

Animus mollitur.

What Seneca Meant

Effort that continues without pause can harden into obligation. When actions aren't periodically reconsidered, they lose responsiveness. Review softens that rigidity by allowing judgment to reassess tone and proportion. Flexibility doesn't come from changing everything—it comes from remaining aware that change remains possible. Persistence becomes strain when effort's never reconsidered.

Why This Still Matters

Long stretches of responsibility often reward endurance alone. Over time, effort can feel heavy simply because it's gone unexamined. Without reflection, persistence risks losing its sense of choice and becoming something carried rather than directed. The weight comes not from the work itself, but from treating it as immovable.

How to Apply This Today

Ongoing effort should feel responsive, not endured. Reflection doesn't require changing course—just checking whether the current path still reflects deliberate choice rather than momentum. That distinction keeps effort sustainable instead of letting it harden into rigid obligation.

"You stay coherent by returning attention to what holds."

Constantia ex attentione manet.

What Seneca Meant

Coherence doesn't happen automatically—it requires periodic return to what matters. Standards, priorities, and sense of self all drift under pressure unless attention's regularly brought back to them. This practice serves as that return. Not transformation, not dramatic insight—just maintenance. A life holds together when someone continues paying attention to whether it still holds.

Why This Still Matters

Modern pressures fragment attention constantly. Without deliberate return to coherence, life becomes reactive—shaped by what's urgent rather than what's important. Days fill with response, weeks blur into months, and somewhere in that rush, the sense of who you intended to be gets lost beneath who circumstances made you become.

Reflection creates that return, helping maintain alignment between intention and action across changing circumstances. It's the practice that keeps everything else from slowly coming apart. Without it, coherence erodes so gradually you don't notice until significant repair is required.

How to Apply This Today

Is daily reflection part of your routine, or does it only happen when problems surface? The practice works best as prevention—catching small drift before it becomes large misalignment. Five minutes of honest review today prevents hours of correction later.

The real question: can you afford to keep moving without it? Most people discover reflection's cost only after paying it—when coherence has eroded enough to require rebuilding rather than simple maintenance.

Chapter 12

Living as a Unified Whole

A life rarely falls apart all at once. It loosens through small inconsistencies—decisions that make sense in isolation but never quite line up, priorities that shift depending on which role you're playing, standards that bend to fit whatever context you're in. Seneca's attentive to this slow fragmentation. He's interested in what allows a life to remain coherent when pressure pulls in competing directions.

This final chapter focuses on integration. The earlier themes—time, emotion, ambition, restraint, reflection—aren't gathered here to be summarized, but to be seen working together. Coherence isn't about perfection or completion. It's about whether decisions relate to one another in a way that feels intelligible, whether priorities remain recognizable across different contexts, whether you're acting from the same center regardless of which part of life demands attention.

What holds a life together, for Seneca, is alignment. When judgment stays consistent, effort doesn't pull in opposing directions. Calm appears as a byproduct rather than a target. The sense of being fragmented—managing multiple selves for different audiences—gradually gives way to something steadier.

These quotes explore what it means for a life to remain coherent over time. What emerges is a view of integrity not as moral perfection, but as internal consistency—being recognizably yourself across changing circumstances.

"A life holds together when its parts answer to the same judgment."

Una ratio vitae.

What Seneca Meant

Coherence depends on shared standards. When decisions in different areas of life arise from the same judgment, effort doesn't contradict itself. You're not maintaining separate standards for work, family, ambition, and rest—each bending to accommodate whatever pressure's currently strongest. You're operating from a single reference point that travels with you across contexts.

This doesn't mean every choice looks identical. It means the reasoning behind choices remains recognizable. The person making decisions at work is the same person making them at home, using the same values, applying the same limits. Unity of judgment is what allows actions, priorities, and responses to make sense together rather than canceling each other out.

Why This Still Matters

Modern life fragments attention constantly. Different roles come with different expectations—work demands one version of you, family another, social settings another. Without a common reference point, these demands collide. You're not inconsistent because you're flawed. You're inconsistent because you're trying to satisfy competing standards that were never meant to coexist.

The result is friction that feels constant even when nothing's visibly wrong. You meet every obligation, yet feel increasingly scattered. The problem isn't the obligations themselves—it's that they're being met by different versions of you operating from different centers.

How to Apply This Today

Notice whether decisions across different areas feel compatible or whether they're pulling against each other. When a choice at work would contradict a value you hold at home, that gap reveals where judgment's fragmenting. Seeing those contradictions early allows you to restore alignment before the tension becomes its own problem.

"You can't hold a life together while holding contradictory standards."

Sibi repugnans nihil efficit.

What Seneca Meant

Internal contradictions consume energy. When you maintain one standard in private and another in public, one for convenience and another for principle, judgment fractures. You're not advancing in any clear direction—you're oscillating between incompatible commitments, each undermining the other. Effort that should be building something coherent instead gets spent managing the tension between conflicting aims.

Why This Still Matters

It's easy to adapt standards to circumstances—being lenient when it suits you, strict when it serves your interests, flexible when pressure mounts. Each adjustment seems reasonable in isolation. But over time, these adjustments accumulate into contradictions you can't reconcile. You've built a life that makes sense only if you don't look at all the pieces together.

How to Apply This Today

Where do your standards shift depending on context? If you'd judge someone else's behavior differently than your own, or if what's acceptable at work wouldn't be acceptable at home, those contradictions are costing you coherence. They don't need dramatic resolution—just acknowledgment and gradual realignment.

"Coherence shows up in whether you recognize yourself across situations."

Vita sibi constat.

What Seneca Meant

A coherent life feels recognizably yours. When you look at decisions made under different pressures, across different contexts, they form a pattern you can see. Not perfection, not completion—just consistency. You're the same person responding to different circumstances, not different people occupying the same life.

This recognition matters. It's the difference between authorship and reaction, between living deliberately and just managing whatever comes next. When choices feel owned rather than forced, even difficulty fits into a larger pattern that makes sense.

Why This Still Matters

Pressure makes life feel reactive. Days fill with response, decisions pile up, momentum replaces intention. Over time, this creates distance from your own direction even while responsibilities are being met. You're efficient, productive, managing everything—and increasingly disconnected from any sense that this life belongs to you.

How to Apply This Today

Reflect briefly on recent choices. Do they form a recognizable pattern, or do they look like accommodations to whoever was asking loudest? When you can trace decisions back to consistent values rather than just reacting to circumstances, that recognition restores authorship. You're not controlling outcomes—you're maintaining coherence regardless of what happens.

"Alignment produces more clarity than intensity ever will."

Concordia animi luciditatem facit.

What Seneca Meant

Intensity drives action but doesn't ensure coherence. You can work harder, push further, add more effort—and still feel scattered if that effort's pulling in competing directions. Alignment does what force can't. When judgment's settled, even moderate effort carries forward without strain because it's not fighting itself.

Clarity emerges from agreement, not exertion. Decisions made from aligned judgment feel lighter because they're not generating internal conflict. You're not spending energy managing contradictions or justifying choices that don't quite fit together.

Why This Still Matters

Pressure rewards urgency and speed, which often leads to bursts of effort that exhaust attention without producing steadiness. You sprint through obligations, collapse briefly, then sprint again. The pace feels necessary, but intensity without alignment creates wear rather than progress. Over time, you're depleting resources without building anything coherent.

How to Apply This Today

Does effort feel driven or guided? Driven effort pushes through resistance by sheer force. Guided effort flows from decisions that already agree with your values. The first exhausts. The second sustains. Treating alignment as the reference point explains why calmer periods often feel more productive than frantic ones—not because you're doing more, but because what you're doing isn't contradicting itself.

"You stay whole by refusing to maintain separate versions of yourself."

Unus esto.

What Seneca Meant

Fragmentation starts innocently—adjusting behavior to fit different contexts, modulating standards to meet different expectations. Each adjustment seems reasonable. But multiply those adjustments across enough situations, and you're not adapting—you're fragmenting. You're maintaining different selves for different audiences, and eventually losing track of which version's actually you.

Why This Still Matters

Modern life encourages context-switching constantly. Professional self, family self, social self—each comes with its own script. The cost of all that switching isn't just cognitive load. It's coherence. When you're a different person in each context, none of those people feel fully real. You're performing competently everywhere while feeling authentic nowhere.

How to Apply This Today

Where are you maintaining separate versions of yourself? Not reasonable flexibility—actual fragmentation. The test is simple: would you be comfortable if all the people in your life saw you in all your contexts? If there's someone you'd hide from someone else, that gap's costing you wholeness. You don't need to be identical everywhere—just recognizably the same person.

"Consistency matters more than resolution."

Constantia plus valet.

What Seneca Meant

Life keeps changing. Conditions rarely resolve cleanly. What allows a life to hold together isn't reaching some final state where everything's settled—it's whether judgment remains recognizable despite ongoing change. Consistency is a living quality, maintained through ordinary choices rather than decisive moments.

Why This Still Matters

Modern pressure frames life as a series of problems to solve. When resolution becomes the measure of progress, ongoing responsibilities feel unfinished. This creates restlessness even in stable circumstances—you're always waiting for the moment when everything finally clicks into place. But coherence doesn't require completion. It requires consistency.

How to Apply This Today

Stop waiting for life to be "resolved" before feeling coherent. The demands won't stop. Circumstances won't settle into perfect alignment. But you can remain consistent regardless—responding from the same center, applying the same standards, maintaining the same priorities even as specifics shift. That consistency is what holds a life together when nothing else does.

"When effort stops pulling in opposite directions, calm appears."

Animus compositus.

What Seneca Meant

Strain often comes from conflicting aims rather than from effort itself. When priorities compete, energy disperses and judgment feels pressured. You're not overwhelmed by the workload—you're exhausted by managing contradictions. Calm emerges when choices no longer cancel each other out, when effort follows a single orientation instead of fighting itself.

Why This Still Matters

You can manage multiple demands that are each reasonable individually. But without alignment, those demands collide. The resulting tension gets experienced as constant urgency, even when there's no actual crisis. You're always feeling behind, always feeling like something's slipping—not because you're failing, but because your efforts are competing rather than cooperating.

How to Apply This Today

Notice where effort feels divided. Which commitments pull against each other? Where does meeting one obligation mean neglecting another? Those conflicts reveal misalignment. The solution isn't always choosing one over the other—sometimes it's realigning both around a shared standard, so they stop contradicting each other and start serving the same direction.

"A life holds together when you recognize it as your own."

Vita sibi adsentitur.

What Seneca Meant

Coherence depends on recognition—being able to see your life as something shaped rather than endured. This doesn't require control over events. It requires acknowledgment of judgment at work within them. When choices feel owned, even difficulty fits into a pattern. You're not being carried by circumstances—you're responding to them from a consistent center.

Why This Still Matters

Momentum can replace intention so gradually you don't notice. Decisions accumulate, responsibilities multiply, and somewhere in that accumulation, you lose track of whether any of this reflects what you actually value or whether you're just managing whatever landed on you. The life's yours in the sense that you're living it—but it doesn't feel like yours in any deeper sense.

How to Apply This Today

Reflect on recent choices. When looking back, can you recognize deliberate judgment at work, or does it look like pure reaction to circumstances? Even choices made under constraint can feel owned if they reflect your values rather than just accommodating pressure. That recognition—"I chose this, even if I didn't choose the circumstances"—is what maintains authorship when control isn't possible.

"Integration isn't dramatic. It's ordinary decisions that don't contradict each other."

Convenientia vitae.

What Seneca Meant

A unified life doesn't require dramatic transformation or perfect alignment. It shows up in ordinary moments—decisions that don't undermine each other, choices that reflect the same values regardless of context, responses that come from the same judgment whether anyone's watching or not. Integration is mundane. It's the quiet accumulation of choices that actually agree rather than secretly contradicting themselves.

Why This Still Matters

We often imagine coherence as something achieved through major life changes—quitting the job, moving cities, starting over. But fragmentation usually doesn't come from one big misalignment. It comes from hundreds of small ones—adjustments that seemed reasonable in the moment but never quite fit together. Integration works the same way: small agreements, accumulated over time, until the life feels recognizably whole.

How to Apply This Today

You don't need to overhaul your life to restore coherence. Start with one day. Make today's decisions agree with each other—same standards across contexts, same values regardless of who's asking, same priorities whether anyone's watching or not. One coherent day doesn't solve everything, but it shows you what integration actually feels like. Then you can build from there.

Notes on Translation and Selection

This book presents Seneca with intention rather than completeness. The passages included prioritize clarity and contemporary relevance—addressing pressures still recognizable: time misused, emotion outpacing judgment, ambition exceeding proportion. Technical discussions and historically specific debates are excluded.

The English translations favor meaning over literalism. Where word-for-word accuracy would obscure Seneca's point or introduce unnecessary formality, phrasing has been adjusted. This reflects how Seneca wrote—direct, compressed, situational. The goal is clarity without modernization or archaism.

Original Latin appears alongside each English rendering to anchor meaning and preserve proportion. What remains is not a complete Seneca, but a usable one.

Seneca's works are in the public domain. Source texts (English and Latin) are freely available online. Scan the QR code below to access the source texts hosted on Project Gutenberg.

Works of Lucius Annaeus Seneca

Thanks

Thank you for spending time with this book. Reading is a quiet commitment, and I don't take it lightly. I hope these pages offered clarity rather than noise, and something useful rather than something loud.

My thanks go to the collaborators at Karma Studio, whose careful work and steady support helped bring this project to completion. I am also grateful to Giulio Vitali, author of *Vox Populi*, for his thoughtful guidance and considered advice throughout the development of this book.

I want to thank my family as well, for their patience and encouragement during the long hours this work required. Their support made that time possible.

If you found this book helpful and feel inclined to do so, leaving an honest review on Amazon would be appreciated. Reviews support independent authors and help other readers decide whether a book like this may be right for them.

Thank you again for reading.

— Richard Lawson